The Archaeology
of Hollywood

The Archaeology of Hollywood

Traces of the Golden Age

PAUL G. BAHN

ROWMAN & LITTLEFIELD
Lanham • Boulder • New York • Toronto • Plymouth, UK

The author attempted to contact all permissions holders with due diligence, so any oversight of permissions can be remedied through the publisher.

Published by Rowman & Littlefield
4501 Forbes Boulevard, Suite 200, Lanham, Maryland 20706
www.rowman.com

10 Thornbury Road, Plymouth PL6 7PP, United Kingdom

British Library Cataloguing in Publication Information Available

Library of Congress Cataloging-in-Publication Data

Bahn, Paul G.
  The archaeology of Hollywood : traces of the golden age / Paul G. Bahn.
    pages cm.
  Includes bibliographical references and index.
  ISBN 978-0-7591-2378-6 (cloth : alk. paper) — ISBN 978-0-7591-2379-3 (electronic) 1. Hollywood (Los Angeles, Calif.)—History. 2. Hollywood (Los Angeles, Calif.)—Social life and customs. 3. Motion picture industry—California—Los Angeles—History. I. Title.
  F869.H74B35 2014
  979.4'94—dc23   2013040684

∞™ The paper used in this publication meets the minimum requirements of American National Standard for Information Sciences—Permanence of Paper for Printed Library Materials, ANSI/NISO Z39.48-1992.

Printed in the United States of America

For Debbie and Jim,
and in memory of Dominique Cazenave

Contents

Acknowledgments

The origins of this book really lie with my mother, who not only transmitted to me her love of history but also took me at an early age to London and Paris. Together we visited Westminster Abbey, St. Paul's, and the three main Paris cemeteries, both of us taking pleasure in seeing the last resting places of so many celebrities of different kinds—rulers, generals, writers, scientists, artists, thespians. . . . Thus began a lifelong hobby which seems morbid to many, but which I have never ceased to find fascinating. One can no longer meet celebrities who have died, so a visit to their graves is the closest one can come to them. It's an opportunity to pay one's respects in some cases and even to say thank you in others. For example, whenever I see their graves, I always give my thanks to Stan Laurel, Oliver Hardy, and Buster Keaton for the enormous pleasure their work has given me. Clayton Moore was one of the heroes of my childhood through my love of *The Lone Ranger* on TV; Charlton Heston was one of the heroes of my youth through his roles in *Ben-Hur* and *El Cid*.

But in common with many people, on my first trip to Los Angeles in 1981 the only tomb that really interested me was that of Marilyn Monroe, still today the most-visited grave in Hollywood. At that time, I knew nothing of the cemeteries of Los Angeles. But on Hollywood Boulevard, quite by chance, I acquired a copy of a privately published book called *The Stars Beyond* (1978, by Jim Perry), which provided an introduction to the main cemeteries and their famous residents. Amazingly, I have never seen another copy of that book since that day, and there were no other such volumes available then—whereas there are many today (see bibliography)—so it seems to have been providence at work. I set about visiting as many of the cemeteries and graves as I could, and I have maintained that habit on all of my many subsequent visits to Los Angeles. In 1986 I even published a guide-map to the Hollywood cemeteries: *Map to the Stars' Graves* (Final Curtain), now long out of print.

Inevitably, in tandem with these cemetery visits, I fell in love with the history of Hollywood and the few remains of its Golden Age—partly through inheriting my mother's passion for history, and partly through my own professional interests as an archaeologist. In the early 1990s I found a kindred spirit in Dominique Cazenave, a French photographer, journalist, and TV producer. He too adored Hollywood history, and together we conceived a plan to produce a book on the "archaeology of Hollywood," combining my text with his photographs. At that time, however, we were simply unable to find a publisher—those we approached either found the subject kitsch or could not envisage how to handle it. Fortunately, times have now changed—but sadly, the change has come too late for Dominique, who died of septicemia in 1998, at the age of only forty-nine. That is why this book is dedicated to his memory. I cannot match the quality of his photographs, but I hope that he would have approved of this volume.

On my first visit to Los Angeles, I was compelled—as a non-driver (a very rare species in that city)—to move around using public transport (mostly buses), which was possible but often quite difficult. On later visits I was fortunate enough to have friends who were willing to drive me to the cemeteries and other sites I wanted to visit. I am supremely grateful to Debbie Stonehouse, without whom this book would simply not have been possible. She has driven me hundreds of miles over the years and has shown amazing tolerance and patience in the face of my "grave activities." I am also indebted to Debbie and her husband Jim for their unfailing hospitality and kindness over the years. I also would like to thank others who provided transport in earlier years: Camille Catalogne, Carolyn Tallent, Lisa Starr, and Debra Bahn. I am grateful to Roger Sinclair, the foremost expert on Hollywood graves, for sharing his knowledge and taking me into an otherwise inaccessible mausoleum. My thanks also to Scott Wilson, another cemetery aficionado, for putting me in touch with Roger. Bill Hyder was kind enough to take me to the Guadalupe Dunes and the Dunes Center. And Dirk Huyge and Luc Delvaux provided useful information on the Egyptian structures and motifs to be found in Hollywood.

Finally, I am deeply grateful to Wendi Schnaufer, who commissioned this book for AltaMira Press/Rowman & Littlefield, and to Andrea Offdenkamp Kendrick, who saw it through to publication.

Paul G. Bahn, July 2013

Introduction

There are a great number of books which deal with Hollywood and its history; they focus on the development of the movie industry, on particular studios, stars, or categories of movie, on gossip, scandal, and nightlife. Yet there has never before been a book on the archaeology of Hollywood.

This may appear a strange notion at first sight; but in fact it is a perfectly legitimate approach to the place. Archaeology is the study of the material traces of our past, and although most people imagine that the subject is concerned only with cavemen, Egyptians, Romans, or Vikings, this is very far from being the case. In fact, archaeology covers all periods, from the days of the earliest humans right up to what happened yesterday: for example, industrial archaeology is a well-established branch of the subject which investigates and preserves the relics of the industrial age; while in Tucson, Arizona, archaeology students for many years carried out the "Garbage Project," delving into garbage cans in an attempt to study in detail what modern American consumers throw away, and in what quantities.

What I have attempted here is a twofold study of Hollywood as an "ancient culture": first, a survey of what little remains of the "Golden Age" of Hollywood; and second, occasional humorous assessments of how a visiting archaeologist from another planet, utterly unfamiliar with the "Hollywood Culture," might interpret some of its more bizarre remains. This is not, therefore, a dry, academic piece of work, but a lighthearted investigation of a place which is still magical to us. I have endeavored to discover what material traces survive, to underline the fact that much of it is neglected, and to point out that unless steps are taken to protect and preserve the little which is left, Hollywood will have irrevocably lost almost all of its past. Future generations would never forgive us if we allowed that to happen.

A joke often told in Europe would have us believe that America is the only culture known in history which evolved from a state of barbarism to one of decadence without passing through a phase of civilization in between. The joke might more aptly be applied to Hollywood, which was transformed very rapidly from a desert settlement to a place which epitomized decadence for the world.

It is certainly justifiable to treat Hollywood as an archaeological "culture"; in fact, it was a very important one, the first in the history of the world which managed to influence virtually every part of the globe with the products of its industry. Film is a very powerful instrument, and the early stars of moving pictures such as William S. Hart, Douglas Fairbanks, Mary Pickford, and Charlie Chaplin were the biggest there have ever been, who were known and worshipped everywhere. The stars of the silent screen spoke a universal language of gesture and expressions, and they were the first performing artists in history whose work was recorded for posterity, thus perpetuating and sometimes magnifying their cult—the cult of Rudolph Valentino, like those of later talking stars Marilyn Monroe and James Dean, is flourishing as never before.

Various movie stars have been accorded the title "King of Hollywood" or "Queen of Hollywood," but in archaeological terms, the performers were more like religious leaders, deified rulers whose reign was upheld through the propagation of a "mythology." But of course it was also upheld, and in some cases destroyed, by the real power of the bureaucrats and administrators: the studio heads and the major directors, and behind them the faceless financiers. These were the real Royal Family—people like Cecil B. DeMille, Louis Mayer, Sam Goldwyn, the Warner Brothers, and many others.

Like any other archaeological culture, Hollywood displayed certain classic features: there was the industrial zone (the studios) where the product was put together before being exported far and wide; the residential areas (Beverly Hills, Bel Air, etc.) where the importance and wealth of different individuals could often be deduced from the size and splendor of their houses and estates; the "play" areas used for rest and recreation, comprising restaurants, bars, clubs, theaters, stores, and so forth; the special "ritual areas" connected with the cult, such as sidewalks decorated with stars, or the display of foot- and handprints and signatures in cement; the monumental structures such as the statues, or the Hollywood sign, designed to reflect the power and well-being of the culture; and, finally, the cemeteries, where the graves, like houses, often provide clues to the social or cult status of the deceased.

The great advantage to the archaeologist in looking at a recent culture of this type is that we know about different individuals and can therefore focus on some of them, looking at the places of significance in their lives: the houses where they lived, died, or were killed; the studios where they did outstanding work; their last resting places.

In short, this book is an offbeat look at a previously neglected aspect of a unique phenomenon, a cotton-candy kingdom which was lighthearted on the surface but all too serious beneath the gloss. Hollywood created kings and gods, raising ordinary folk to unprecedented heights; it also destroyed people and killed people. Sometimes it took pleasure in subjecting the same individual to both extremes. When the harsh side of Hollywood is remembered, an analogy is often made with Babylon; but perhaps a far more appropriate model is Ancient Rome at its height, with the studio heads as ruthless, all-powerful emperors, issuing decrees and hatching plots from their luxurious poolside couches. It is no accident that they were also called "movie moguls" after the equally despotic rulers of the East.

Sadly, the illusion is now a thing of the past. Like a movie which flickers vividly on a giant screen, only to vanish abruptly into darkness, Hollywood is no more. Its industrial zone is now full of TV studios, its residential areas largely occupied by TV producers, rock stars, and second-rate actors. Most major movies are now made on location elsewhere. The glamor of the place has faded, the fakery has become more apparent, and sleaze stalks "Hollyweird" Boulevard. Only when a premiere is held at Grauman's Chinese Theatre, with floodlights piercing the sky, does a pale shadow of the old dream become visible, like a son et lumière at the Pyramids or the Acropolis.

There is a huge and ever-growing interest in old Hollywood around the world, as the early stars dwindle to a very elderly few. A dedicated network of enthusiasts has undertaken the vital task of rescuing the product of the "Hollywood Culture"—all too many of those precious images on inflammable nitrate celluloid have already decayed or been destroyed, but the remainder are being preserved and restored, and rediscovered by new generations.

Inevitably the new army of admirers will also be interested in the background to the product and the everyday lives of those who made the movies. That is why I set out to track down the material remains of the grand old days before they too are torn down to make yet more parking lots or supermarkets, without even a commemorative plaque about the history made on those sites. It seems strange that America should neglect the very part of its short history which epitomizes America for the world, and which carried its cultural influence far and wide.

This is why it is perhaps inevitable that the author of such a book should be from the Old World. Americans may be too near to the subject to appreciate it fully; it is no accident that certain American directors and comedians became huge successes in Europe before their own country realized their worth. In the same way, the Eiffel Tower epitomizes Paris for the world, but few Parisians notice it any more—even fewer bother to visit the monument. It is the foreign tourists who frequent the tower, just as it is those who live far away from Hollywood who tend to appreciate it the most.

More than nine million tourists come to Hollywood each year because they want to experience the places where movie stars lived and worked and died. This is modern America's history, its heritage. Yet most of it has gone forever.

Nevertheless, there is hope for what little remains of old Hollywood. A nonprofit organization in Los Angeles known as Hollywood Heritage (www.hollywoodheritage.org), which has now existed for over thirty years, is "dedicated to preservation of the historic built environment in Hollywood and to education about the early film industry and the role its pioneers played in shaping Hollywood's industry." The organization has played a significant role in the preservation of numerous historic cultural monuments, and it monitors the Hollywood Register of Historic Places. One of its great successes was the preservation and relocation of the Lasky-DeMille Barn (see chapter 4).

It should be noted that, as used in this volume, the name "Hollywood" actually encompasses a large area from Los Angeles to the San Fernando Valley and the Pacific Ocean. It denotes not the small geographical community within the city of Los Angeles, but the entertainment industry in its broader sense.

This book is part history, part archaeology, part personal reminiscence, and part whimsy. It in no way aspires to compete with the major studies of Hollywood's past by Bruce Torrence or Gregory Paul Williams, which are strongly recommended to those wishing to delve deeper into the subject.

ONE

The Prehistory of Hollywood

There is abundant evidence of habitation by Native American peoples in the greater Los Angeles area, including the San Fernando Valley, for at least ten thousand years.

The most important site for studying the area's remote past is undoubtedly the La Brea tar pits, one of the most famous fossil sites in the world—located not in some desert but in the very center of Los Angeles, surrounded by skyscrapers. Rancho La Brea used to be a Mexican land grant near the small Pueblo de Los Angeles. It was mined for natural asphalt in the past, but it has also yielded a wealth of animal fossils up to 44,000 years old: mammoths, sabre-toothed cats, packs of dire wolves, and numerous birds that had been trapped in the tar and subsequently entombed. Many other creatures shared their fate, from small insects to giant ground sloths.

At first the numerous bones found in the deposits were dismissed as those of modern domestic or wild animals. It was only in the 1870s that the bones were recognized as being from fossil animals, and serious excavations were first carried out from 1906 to 1913. The work is dirty and grueling even today—the stuff has the consistency of badly made fudge, and the color of high-quality licorice. Small trowels are needed to scrape the crumbly asphalt and transfer it to buckets. Everything has to be examined in case it contains microfossils such as bugs.

Since 1977 some of the La Brea remains have been beautifully displayed in the George C. Page Museum on the site, a satellite of the Natural History Museum of Los Angeles County. Designed to be both a research and educational facility, its fossil storage areas and paleontology laboratory are both on full view so that the public can observe the cleaning, preparation, cataloging, and study of the fossils. Children can see mounted skeletons and animated models, test their strength against the pull of asphalt, and touch the massive, asphalt-soaked bone of a giant ground sloth. The outside of the museum has huge cast-fiberglass friezes depicting scenes with Ice Age fauna, while a lake features life-size figures of Columbian mammoths illustrating one of the many dramas that occurred in this natural trap. Pits and pools still bubble and reek of pitch.

All the bones come from the Rancho La Brea deposits, and they owe their brown color to natural staining by the asphalt. Mostly dating from 44,000 to 4,000 years ago, the remains even include single-celled plants, pollen seeds, leaves and wood, snail and clam shells, insects and spiders, fish, frogs and toads, and snakes and turtles, as well as the birds and mammals mentioned above, all of which help to produce a detailed picture of the changing environment and climate during these millennia, and of the diversity of Ice Age life. Literally millions of specimens of vertebrate and invertebrate fossils have been recovered in excavations, representing 140 species of plants and over 420 species of animals—over one hundred tons of remains, making this by far the richest source of Ice Age fossils in the world. Huge quantities of bones continue to be excavated there today.

This area was a natural trap. Asphalt from an underground oil deposit seeped to the surface in warm summer weather, and

Life-size figure of Columbian mammoth at the La Brea tar pits.

its puddles were probably masked by a coating of wind-blown leaves, sand, and dust. Unwary animals—especially bison—then got trapped in the sticky goo. It is reckoned that a depth of just 1.5 inches would be enough to immobilize an animal the size of a horse. The trapped animals' struggles and subsequent death attracted carnivores and scavengers, like big cats, wolves, vultures, and condors, which got stuck in their turn. Others would have been trapped when the pools were occasionally covered with water, and unsuspecting animals waded in for a drink. The bodies rapidly decayed, and the bones became saturated with asphalt and sank into the mire. During the winter, cooler weather solidified the asphalt, and streams of rainwater deposited a layer of sediment over the exposed bones. The warm weather of the next summer then dried the streams and liquefied the asphalt, and the trap was reset.

The most exciting find from an archaeological point of view was the discovery of one human, La Brea Woman, in the deposits. Her skull and a dozen skeletal elements are thought to be about nine thousand years old; she was 4 feet 8 inches tall and about eighteen years old. The skull and partial skeleton of a dog, possibly a pet, were beside her, and she seemed to have been buried ceremonially. A deliberately damaged *mano* (grinding stone) was with her, which reflects a burial practice of southern California aboriginal peoples. A hologram of the woman is on show in the museum. Her broken skull and jaw led many to believe she had been hit with a blunt instrument, and was thus a murder victim, but it is possible that the damage occurred during a reburial or excavation.

More than fifty well-preserved artifacts have been recovered from La Brea, ranging from approximately 9,000 to almost 4,000 years old. They feature tools for food-gathering and preparation (hunting implements, grinding stones), ceremonial or symbolic items (e.g., an enigmatic, cogged stone, seen by some as utilitarian, perhaps the weight for a digging stick or fishing net), and tools for collecting and mining asphalt. Personal items include a wooden spatula-shaped hairpin, another hairpin carved from deer bone, and ornaments of bone and shell. Several wooden atlatl (spear-thrower) parts have also survived. The mining tools are the most common—many shells of scallop and other marine mollusks (probably used as containers), and wedges made of deer and elk antler, which were probably fitted to handles and used as picks. Since elk were never present in the region, their antlers must have been obtained by trade from the southern San Joaquin Valley.

The intermediate (3,000–1,000 years ago) and late prehistoric (AD 1000–1769) periods are represented by double-drilled abalone shell pendants, awls, and also, once again, shell scoops and elk antler wedges. Aboriginal camps probably always existed in the vicinity of the deposits, involved not only in asphalt mining and exploitation but also in hunting and fishing, and perhaps ceremonial activities.

The local Native Americans had many uses for the asphalt. With stone tools they cut small planks from available trees, bored holes in them, and tied them together with strips of hide to form boats. Asphalt was then used to caulk the cracks between the planks. Baskets were caulked in the same way so that they could hold water heated by hot stones, and thus cook acorn meal. Stone implements were also fastened to wooden handles with sinew and asphalt.

The first written accounts of La Brea (which is Spanish for "tar") date to 1769 and were produced by members of an expedition led by Gaspar de Portolá, the governor of lower California, as the expedition traveled through the valley of Los Angeles on its way to Monterey to take over all of California for

Spain. By 1828, the springs were included in a land grant called Rancho La Brea, and the asphalt was being used to waterproof the roofs of adobe houses in the area—large solidified pieces were broken off with an axe and laid on the flat roofs on top of a layer of earth. It also waterproofed canoes and greased wagon wheels. In later years the material was sold as fuel, mined for use as a preservative for pipes and railroad ties, and even shipped to San Francisco to pave the streets.

The best-known tribes of the region were the Gabrieliño (or Gabrieleño) and, just to the north, the Chumash. The former were so named by the Spanish after the San Gabriel Archangel Mission, which was intended to look after the Indians' spiritual well-being. The tribes were not nomadic and lived in villages (indeed one major communal trading village, Cabueg-na, now lies beneath Universal Studios), maintaining social and trading contacts between settlements, and they intermarried. Being hunter-gatherers, they had plentiful sources of food due to the mild climate, the region's fertility, and their proximity to the ocean. As a consequence, they seem to have had lots of free time to devote to crafts such as basketry and the carving of bone and shell.

Chumash baskets have long been admired for their quality and design. Before the European arrivals, they were highly valued and traded far and wide among native tribes. The best-known form was a sturdy coiled basket, created from a spiraling base composed of three thin stalks of rush sewn together with split strands of the same rushes. They were usually a natural straw color, with geometric designs created by applying a dark dye to them. They were an essential part of everyday life for the Chumash, being used for carrying, storing, and transporting. Baskets also served as gifts and were employed in ceremonies and trade, as well as for gathering, storing, and serving food.

Tightly woven specimens could even hold water, and hence be used in cooking, when hot stones were added to the water and food inside them. Asphalt, as mentioned above, was also a help in waterproofing, and certainly this material was traded throughout southern California for that purpose, as well as for its use as an adhesive.

The staple foods in the region included acorns and wild grass seeds. Acorns were gathered and dried; then, once the shell had been removed, the nuts could be ground into a flour. Native plants were also used for medicinal and religious purposes, with sage, for example, being burned during some rituals.

The ancient inhabitants of southern California were very skilled fishers and hunters, and their cultures and social structures were rich and complex. They also had a highly developed ritual life and a remarkable tradition of colorful rock paintings featuring geometric shapes, zoomorphs, and sun-like designs.

Trade between villages and between tribes was common, involving a wide range of commodities such as animal skins, spear points made of obsidian and chert, pigments for body paint, baskets, food, and ornamental objects. It is known that one rite, the "Great Mourning Ceremony," involved honoring important deceased people by dancing and singing and then destroying objects—by breaking and/or burning—to release the "spirits of the objects" so that the dead could use them in the afterlife. This is probably one reason why so many stone artifacts that have been found in southern California are broken and burned—the objects were "killed" in such ceremonies (as we saw in the case of the La Brea Woman's grinding stone).

The Gabrieliño people had cult practices which included drinking an infusion of the toloache plant (*Datura inoxia*)—also known as jimsonweed—a hallucinogen which can produce color visions, unconsciousness, and even death if a dose is too concentrated. Boys would take this drug when being initiated into adulthood or cult membership, and they had to be carefully watched by elders during their many hours of unconsciousness. While under the drug's influence, the boys would have a vision and thus gain "power" of some kind, such as becoming courageous or becoming skillful and successful hunters. The taking of drugs by the region's later "Hollywood Culture" thus had native precedents! Alas, in recent years many young people, having heard of jimsonweed's effects, have tried it as a thrill—without realizing just how poisonous and dangerous it is, or that there is no effective antidote—and a number of deaths have resulted.

The oldest ethnohistoric document about the California Indians of the region dates to 1543, when a Portuguese captain, Juan Rodríguez Cabrillo, led an expedition northward from San Diego Bay to take possession of the land for the king of Spain. Another forty years then passed before other Europeans visited California. Inevitably their arrival brought new diseases—smallpox, measles, diphtheria, and so forth—which had a dramatic impact on the native populations. Even before the Spanish settlement of southern California, diseases had already reached the region along the old Aztec trade routes.

In the eighteenth century, the Spanish crown felt it a religious duty to combat heathenism and bring Catholicism to as many native peoples as possible. Only this, it was thought, would turn immoral and ignorant non-Christians into true human beings. The Franciscan order was chosen to establish missions in California, starting in San Diego in 1769 and then moving north. In the Hollywood area, the Franciscans picked the biggest, most prosperous native community, known as Yang-na, and turned it into *El Pueblo de la Reyna de Los Angeles* (The village of the Queen of the Angels).

Unfortunately, the Mission Era caused drastic alterations to the native cultures and further reduced the populations through diseases, hard labor, and harsh conditions. The missions were secularized in 1834 through Mexican independence. By the mid-nineteenth century, with statehood and the 1848 California Gold Rush, most Native Americans were gone from this region. Some probably left the area to join other tribes, and others seem to have disappeared into the waves of new settlers.

Mexico had divided the Hollywood basin into two enormous ranchos, La Brea and Los Feliz. They were full of parks, cornfields, orchards, and vineyards, and they had plenty of fresh water. This explains why there is a street called Vine in Hollywood, and indeed, in the early nineteenth century, wine was the main industry of the new township of Los Angeles. At that time, the Hollywood area was called Nopalera, after the nopal, a kind of Mexican cactus that was common there.

In 1850, California became an American state, and a few years later the first house was built in Nopalera, an adobe-and-wood dwelling amid tall sycamores located near what is now Franklin Avenue and Outpost Drive. Its roof was insulated, naturally enough, with pitch from the La Brea deposits. Through the 1850s and 1860s, more homesteads sprang up, and cattle herds and flocks of sheep also arrived.

So much for the earliest inhabitants of this part of southern California. It is now time to turn to the period which really interests us here: that of the "Hollywood Culture."

TWO

Why Hollywood?

The Historical Background

This simple title actually encompasses two important questions which, though different, are closely intertwined: Why did the motion picture industry develop in this particular place, and What is the origin of the name "Hollywood"? The name and its connotations have become so entrenched in popular culture that few people, including those who visit the place, ever pause to ask themselves why a desert environment such as this should be named "Hollywood" rather than "Sagebrush" or "Tumbleweed." It is not generally known that we owe this magical name to a chance meeting on a train; and that a number of French people and—ironically—a banning of liquor were in large measure responsible for the first settlement of movie folk here.

It has been said that you can live your whole life in Los Angeles without any awareness of the city's rich history. Raymond Chandler called Los Angeles "a city with all the personality of a paper cup." It is a place that invented itself out of nothing: at

CHAPTER TWO

first sight there is no reason for it to be here at all—no river, no port, no highway crossroads. Everything is self-made. But why?

Apart from the Pleistocene events at the nearby Rancho La Brea tar pits (see chapter 1), the area's earliest claim to fame is that, in 1847, the peace treaty ending the U.S.-Mexican War was signed at an old adobe house outside Los Angeles, the Casa de Adobe de Cahuenga, later known as "The Outpost," which had been founded by eleven families in 1781 as the Pueblo de Nuestra Señora la Reina de Los Angeles (1903 Outpost Drive, at the intersection of Outpost and Hillside). Unfortunately, the house was destroyed in the 1920s for a housing development. Another notable event, the last battle between Indians and early Californians in the region, on Rancho San Antonio in 1852, is

Plaque marking the site of the last battle between Indians and early Californians, Beverly Hills.

marked by a plaque at the corner of Chevy Chase and Benedict Canyon Drive in Beverly Hills.

Southern California really began to develop in the late 1870s as Midwesterners flowed in on the Southern Pacific Railroad which had recently been completed, and this continued in the 1880s when the Santa Fe arrived. In 1870, the population of Los Angeles was 5,000; by 1880 it was 11,000, and only ten years later it was almost 100,000. Inevitably, the growth of the railway system was accompanied by the selling of real estate, and by the 1890s the previous enormous Mexican land grants had been subdivided into many lucrative residential lots. Writers and artists were paid to produce early hype, that is, brochures and posters, to sing the praises of the area and thus attract thousands of visitors. One such brochure of 1906 claimed

> unequalled and unrivalled in all lands . . . Los Angeles, the metropolis of this Southern Empire, is the mecca to which all tourists go, and from which they take the many trips to the varied and interesting places and points of interest thereto . . . No city of the West suggests such picturesque opportunities and sightseeing possibilities as Los Angeles, or City of Our Lady, the Queen of the Angels, telling of the past, a time of missions and siestas and a future of activity and metropolitan advancement.

Another ploy was to present the area as a sanatorium and health farm, and so numerous people came from the East and Midwest in search of relief through healing sunshine from a wide range of ailments such as tuberculosis, asthma, and other respiratory illnesses. Even today, despite the smog, southern California still attracts people in search of curative, dry warmth.

In the early twentieth century, southern California con-stituted an exotic landscape of oil wells, citrus groves, and a

Western lifestyle. Hollywood was still a nineteenth-century town, with a few twentieth-century accessories—it was a small community of mostly Protestant Midwesterners in Victorian houses strung out along broad, tree-shaded streets. It was basically a small, though ever-growing suburb of Los Angeles, into which it was incorporated in 1910. There were increasing numbers of automobiles, and the world's most extensive electrical transit system.

In 1883, a certain Harvey Henderson Wilcox, a wealthy real estate practitioner and ardent prohibitionist from Topeka, Kansas, had come west to Los Angeles, arriving on the new Atchison, Topeka and Santa Fe Railroad. He and his wife Daeida used to take carriage rides out to the surrounding countryside, seeking some relief from the dirty, loud, and populous city. They became especially fond of the Cahuenga Valley, with its sheltered canyons, ocean views, and cool breezes, so they purchased a large piece of land extending from what is now Gower Street to Whitley Avenue, and from Sunset Boulevard to Franklin Avenue.

It was Daeida who, during a fateful train journey to Ohio, chatted with a wealthy woman named Mrs. Hendricks (or Mrs. Peck in some accounts) and learned that her farm in Illinois (or summer home in another version) was called Hollywood. Mrs. Wilcox liked the name, and accordingly rechristened the Cahuenga Valley–Wilcox Ranch. An alternative story is that the area gained its name from an abundance of toyon (or "Christmas berry," *Heteromeles arbutifolia*), a holly-like shrub with serrated evergreen leaves and red berries which were popular as Christmas decorations.

Whether or not the new name of Hollywood was inappropriate from an environmental point of view, it suited its destiny—after all, it is hard to imagine the world talking of "the Cahuenga film industry"; and "Hooray for Wilcox" would have made a lousy title for a song.

Of course, these names do live on in adjacent streets running across Hollywood and Sunset Boulevards; Mr. Wilcox christened them when he laid out the town—being obsessed with real estate, he subdivided the area around the ranch on a map, and distributed copies to real estate agents. Tourists were already coming because the Cahuenga Valley, known as the "Frostless Belt," was famous for its very impressive yields of oranges (hence Orange Avenue, commemorating an orange grove where Hollywood High School now stands) and especially lemons, groves of which stretched across the area. This was a crucial crop since scurvy was common in the gold-rush period, and farmers could harvest nine crops per year. Many visitors liked the area so much that they bought plots, and prices more than doubled in only three months. The quiet little town of Hollywood became known for "sun, space and somnolence." As the population grew, water became more of a problem, and increasing numbers of deep wells had to be sunk.

Quite rapidly, the real estate boom collapsed, and in 1887 the Wilcoxes had to repay many people who backed out of their purchases. They were then compelled to sell their luxurious home in Los Angeles and move to Hollywood themselves, to a modest farmhouse on the northwest corner of Prospect Avenue (now Hollywood Boulevard) and Cahuenga—the site is at 1721 Cahuenga Boulevard. They laid out a grid of streets, began to grade roads with gravel, and continued their efforts to sell lots. It was obvious to the farsighted that buying land here would be a good investment as inevitably the future would bring more people, and more homes and businesses, and hence property values were certain to rise. But as yet, of course, nobody had the slightest inkling of the particular industry which would transform the place so completely.

Wilcox died in his house in 1891. His widow was only twenty-nine. Ten years later, having remarried in 1894, she sold the house and its grounds to Paul de Longpré, a famous French painter of flowers, for three paintings. De Longpré had come to Los Angeles ostensibly because flowers in New York were expensive and insufficiently varied! His palatial home and beautifully kept flower gardens became Hollywood's first great tourist attraction, apart from the fruit groves, and, amazingly, thousands of people visited them every year. De Longpré's legendary hospitality, especially to newspapermen, ensured widespread fame for him and considerable publicity for Hollywood. He died in 1911, though his name lives on in De Longpre Park. Alas, his house and gardens were destroyed, and they were replaced by a theater and a parking lot. Mrs. Wilcox (later Mrs. Beveridge), the "Mother of Hollywood," died in 1914 at her beautiful home at 6467 Hollywood Boulevard (a bank now occupies the site);

The de Longpré house (postcard).

she is buried next to Harvey Henderson Wilcox in Hollywood Memorial Park (now known as Hollywood Forever).

In August 1903, Hollywood officially became the "City of Hollywood," although it only had a population of seven hundred. A police station was set up, manned by two officers who eventually progressed from horseback to riding bicycles. Their main work involved drunks, cars zooming down Sunset Boulevard at top speed, people driving animal herds down the main avenues, and children throwing lemons at the police. Not all of these are still problems today!

By 1909, the population had reached 4,000, and not only water but sewage had grown into a serious problem. Los Angeles—once a tiny pueblo but now a city of 100,000—refused to share its water unless Hollywood was part of the city. As this was the only solution, in 1910 Hollywood voted to become a district—essentially a suburb—of Los Angeles and lost its independence. That same year, Prospect Avenue's name was officially changed to Hollywood Boulevard, and its eastern end was curved south to join Sunset, which was the main thoroughfare to Los Angeles.

Wilcox had sold property at the northwest corner of Sunset Boulevard and Gower Street to another Frenchman, Louis Blondeau, and his family. Like many residents of Hollywood—often folks from the Midwest living out their retirement in the sun—Wilcox was a prohibitionist, and Blondeau therefore had to agree not to operate a saloon on this property. But when Wilcox died, liquor flowed, and business boomed—until the good people of Hollywood passed an ordinance which forbade the sale of liquor. This is why Madame Blondeau, in 1911—to the horror of the nearby Methodist church's parishioners—leased the roadhouse for $30 a month to some people from the Centaur Film Company of Bayonne, New Jersey, who were seeking a permanent California base. The tavern and adjacent stables, corral, and bungalow became the Nestor Studio, Hollywood's first, which made mostly one-reel Westerns and comedies. The corral was used for horses needed in the Westerns, the bungalow for offices. The site, at 6101–6121 Sunset Boulevard, was bought in 1937 by CBS, which demolished everything to make way for a $2 million radio station.

The movie industry had already been flourishing for years, with films being produced all over America. New York was the center, though many filmmakers moved to Florida during the New York winters. But eventually a number of companies made the long journey west in search of better filmmaking conditions and to escape Thomas Edison's attempts to monopolize the entire industry. The Selig Polyscope Company, for example, based in Chicago, sent people in 1907 to shoot scenes for *The Count of Monte Cristo* at the coastal cliffs of La Jolla and to investigate Los Angeles and Colorado as possible bases, and they chose the former. In 1909 the company rented an empty Chinese laundry at Eighth and Olive streets for use as offices and dressing rooms, and on a stage built next door it filmed *The Heart of a Race Tout*, the first movie ever made completely in California. That same year the Selig Studio was built in Edendale (located at 1845 Glendale—the site has been razed). Other companies set up permanent studios near Oakland, and in Santa Barbara, Santa Monica, Long Beach, and downtown Los Angeles.

In 1910, the Biograph Film Company from New York rented an acre of downtown Los Angeles and began to film one-reelers. One of these, among the very first films shot in Hollywood, titled *Love among the Roses*, was made in a day in de Longpré's flower garden. It featured a fifteen-year old Mary Pickford, and its director and producer was none other than David Wark Griffith, soon to be better known as D. W. Griffith!

One group of studios (including Universal) settled around Sunset Boulevard in Hollywood; but the citizens brought in a zoning ordinance to prevent more studios being built, with the result that Hollywood never became the center of film production, contrary to popular belief. It remained a quiet, attractive suburb, with only one policeman, who usually stood at the corner of Hollywood and Vine (still an area needing law enforcement!). Movie people came in to rent hotel rooms or to buy houses, and eventually the suburb gave its name in popular parlance to the whole film-producing area and to the movie industry in general.

What were the attractions of California in those days for pioneer moviemakers? This was, after all, still a frontier area, four days by train from New York, which, with Chicago, remained the financial nerve center of the industry. California lacked many of the amenities taken for granted in the big cities; its small towns were surrounded by raw desert. Sunset Boulevard had been an old cattle trail, and a bridle path ran down its center because there were few cars, and horses were still an important means of transport; indeed, many of the earliest studios had hitching rails outside.

But the advantages outweighed the shortcomings. Perhaps most important, there was warmth, and sunshine for about 350 days per year, which permitted virtually uninterrupted filming without lights, not just on location but also in studio sets open to the sky. The light was good, an important factor for the slow film used; the backgrounds were clear and sharp in those smog-free days; and the scenery was varied and spectacular—within a short distance one had ocean, desert, lush valleys, mountains, and rugged rocks. A common Latin phrase in old archaeological studies was *ex oriente lux*, the notion that civilization (*lux*, meaning "light" or "culture") came from the East (*ex oriente*)—but where the "Hollywood Culture" was concerned, people came *ex oriente* to take advantage of the *lux*!

In 1913 the Owens Valley aqueduct opened, which ensured a massive supply of water, and the Port of Los Angeles at San Pedro opened to commercial and tourist traffic—two projects which further stimulated the development of the region and helped expand the population. Another major consideration was that land was cheap. Further, Los Angeles was a nonunionized town, and labor costs—thanks to plenty of Mexicans and Asians—were far lower than in New York. So extras were cheap too, and at first many locals even worked for free, for the fun of the experience. Extras were generally paid $1 per day—there was no overtime thanks to the absence of unions, and so work was done on Sundays or holidays for the same fee—and before casting organizations arose, people simply had to turn up for work at the studio gates.

From 1910 to 1920, the population of Hollywood shot up from 5,000 to 36,000, a rise of 720 percent, and by 1929 it was 157,000! After World War I, a good wage was $15 to $18 per week, but it became well known that some people in Hollywood were earning $3,000 per week and living in mansions. Hence constant hordes of people headed west to try their luck at breaking into this world. By 1920, 40 million Americans were going to the movies every week, and the movie business was employing thousands of people (the total payroll was $25 million per year). Films had thus become the world's most successful product, the dominant form of mass entertainment.

The arrival of these droves of "movies," as the filmmakers were known by the locals, became a matter of grave concern to the retired gentlefolk of Hollywood and other towns, who often shunned the high-spirited newcomers like lepers. Signs saying "No Movies" appeared in the windows of places to rent. This was somewhat understandable, as these renters included a lot of questionable and rough characters and vagabonds who often skipped town without paying or who damaged property. In addition, the moviemaking often interfered with normal traffic. And there was a lot of film-burning going on: the only way of getting rid of unwanted film—rejected scenes, outtakes—was to burn it, in order to recover the silver in it, and this caused a nasty smell. Meanwhile, Hollywood's remaining lemon groves were being remorselessly ripped out and destroyed. But any ill feeling on the part of the Los Angeles area authorities was doused when, in 1915, it was revealed that the film industry was already spending $5 million per year on salaries, and employing in excess of twelve thousand people in the region. Within two more years the workforce had risen to twenty thousand, making Hollywood the undisputed moviemaking capital of the world. In other words, by 1917 moviemaking had become Hollywood's foremost and most lucrative industry, and this industry was making more movies than anywhere else in the United States.

Gradually Hollywood also came to outstrip its rivals elsewhere. World War I had a truly devastating effect on moviemaking in Europe—which until then had been tremendously successful in France, Italy, Sweden, and Germany—while winter power shortages in New York in 1919 also led more people to head west. In 1921 no fewer than 854 feature films were made in Hollywood, a hitherto unprecedented output. By 1927 Hollywood was making an average of 700 silent feature films a year.

In short, there was a substantial migration of people westward, and industrialists gradually displaced the orange growers and farmers who had previously reigned supreme here. The "Hollywood Culture" had thus begun by the early years of the twentieth century, and it was rapidly to flood the world with its products—one of the first cultures ever to do so. All over the world, people gobbled up these products; they provided a new form of drama that appealed to people who would never have thought of entering a real theater, even if they could afford a ticket. Films were a new way of telling stories, especially to people who did not read much, if at all, and whose everyday lives had no luxury or glamor. Being silent, the first movies were a universal kind of narrative, and especially so in America with its huge new populations of immigrants who knew little or no English. So this rapidly became the world's first mass entertainment.

There were also unforeseen economic effects, as movies became the dominant cultural force on the planet, and hence products used in the movies became "must-haves" for the audience—clothing fashions, hat styles, cars, and so forth. For example, an early movie starring Gloria Swanson and Conrad Nagel needed a bottle of perfume for some important scenes, so a propman bought an oddly shaped black bottle of perfume called "Christmas Night." Once the movie appeared, the American public bought a million bottles of this perfume that was hitherto unknown! It was movie stars like Greta Garbo, Katharine Hepburn, Joan Crawford, Lupe Velez, Marlene Dietrich, and Barbara Stanwyck who caused a scandal and then a craze by wearing slacks. An advertisement of the time for Hollywood Boulevard comprised a large star made up of the faces of hundreds of movie stars with the slogans "They shop on Hollywood Boulevard and dictate the fashions of the world" and "Hollywood Boulevard, 'Style Center of the World.'"

But this was a two-way street because it was the public who made the stars. Movie producers offered a "menu," but it was the ticket buyers who chose the dishes. This great industry was utterly dependent on the whims and fads of the consumer. Even today, no matter how much a film costs, how lavish the sets, how intriguing the story, if the public stays away, the film is considered a flop.

In 1928 Max Factor, a Russian immigrant and pioneer of screen makeup, moved his successful cosmetics business from downtown Los Angeles to a storage building at 1666–1668 North Highland Avenue, immediately south of Hollywood Boulevard, which he turned into a glamorous art-deco palace with separate rooms for blondes (opened by Jean Harlow), brunettes (Claudette Colbert), and redheads (Ginger Rogers). The building has now become the Hollywood History Museum. His makeup products and styles had a tremendous influence on the women of America and beyond. Not far away, the Westmores opened a beauty salon and barbershop on Sunset Boulevard, near Highland, and their hairstyles likewise influenced the nation.

Another important consequence was the arrival of tourists en masse, in ever-growing numbers, always hoping to spot a star—which was a very common occurrence in those early days. Stars could be seen walking along or driving on the streets, sitting in hotels, eating in restaurants, or dancing in clubs. Entrepreneurs in cars took tourists on the first tours of the stars' homes in Hollywood and Beverly Hills. Tabloid journalism exploded, as the public's insatiable appetite for trivia and news—factual or fictional—about their favorite stars took hold. Rapidly Hollywood turned into the most publicized place on earth, and its press corps grew to become the third biggest in the United States, after those of New York and Washington, DC. In the press corps' heyday, more than three hundred journalists covered Hollywood, and gossip—whether accurate or invented—became a major industry for the first time.

Conversely, poverty also appeared—in 1921 it was estimated that three thousand movie hopefuls were starving in Hollywood, so prostitution was inevitably rampant, with brothels filled with very attractive girls located along Fountain Avenue and Sunset Boulevard. The girls, like numerous waitresses in town, were earning a living as best they could, biding their time until they got their big break. Alcohol problems also soared, along with the use of narcotics. The town filled with con men, chiselers, hoodlums, and touts. There were fraudulent acting schools, and after the arrival of the talkies, fraudulent teachers of diction and voice. By the 1930s it was said that Hollywood had more racketeers than Chicago, shady characters keen to extract money from the disillusioned and hopeless hordes of would-be stars, fake agents and producers, psychic healers, mystics, and (during Prohibition) bootleggers. Mobsters appeared who wanted to infiltrate the studio unions that were forming and thus control the movie industry. After the war, however, once Benjamin "Bugsy" Siegel had built the Flamingo Hotel and Casino in Las Vegas, many of Hollywood's gangsters moved their operations out to Nevada.

As commercialism grew, it directly affected Hollywood Boulevard. It had long ago been planted with pepper trees by Harvey Wilcox, trees which provided welcome shade. But they blocked store signs, so in 1923, despite a campaign to save them led by Mary Pickford, these beautiful old trees were felled and uprooted. Other obstacles to progress, such as the de Longpré house and Mrs. Wilcox/Beveridge's home, were also demolished at this time to make way for yet another movie theater. More and more roads were paved—in 1926 Hollywood had ten miles of paved thoroughfares, but by the end of 1927 there were two hundred miles. Rush-hour traffic was already a nightmare by this period.

Banking also became of huge importance as the movie industry involved hundreds of millions of dollars. Whereas early Hollywood had only two banks, by the early 1920s there were

The First National Bank's tower at Hollywood and Highland; to the right is the former Montmartre Café.

thirty-three, and they included the First National Bank of Los Angeles, located on the northeast corner of Hollywood Boulevard and Highland Avenue, a building whose elegant tower is still one of the most recognizable landmarks in the city.

The late 1920s dealt a double blow to Hollywood and the movie industry; the arrival of the talkies destroyed the careers of quite a few silent stars, while the crash of 1929 affected everyone, wiping out the invested fortunes of stars and moviemakers alike and the savings of many lesser mortals. Mass unemployment hit the town—in 1930, of the 17,000 extras registered with Central Casting, only 30 worked for more than three days! On the other hand, the Great Depression took some time to hit Hollywood since money continued to flow in because all over the country the new masses of unemployed spent a lot of time watching movies: in New York, the streets around Time Square had to be closed to traffic every evening because of the massive crowds going to the movies. But hard times did arrive within a few years—many studios went under, as did numerous retail businesses.

As things recovered after the Depression, one solution adopted for traffic congestion was the construction of new roads and freeways, including Hollywood Parkway, which cut through some of the most beautiful neighborhoods such as Whitley Heights, destroying numerous fine and historic homes in the process, including Rudolph Valentino's former house at 6776 Wedgewood Place, in which he had lived from 1924 to 1925. Freeway construction recommenced and increased markedly after World War II. Bulldozers also swept away numerous fine old dwellings, replacing them with boring, high-density apartment buildings with few amenities and absentee landlords.

By the late 1960s and 1970s Hollywood had become a byword for sleaze. It was filled with shady characters, gangs cruising the streets, addicts, transvestites, sex shops, and massage parlors. It was a center for drugs and prostitution and pornography, and its crime rate was double that of the rest of Los Angeles. Eventually in the late 1970s and early 1980s, Hollywood's chamber of commerce and the Los Angeles Police Department attempted a series of comeback cleanups of the town. But from 1980 to 1981 the murder rate almost doubled, while arrests for narcotics offenses more than doubled. One particularly tragic loss occurred in 1983 when vandals set fire to the Hollywood Branch Library on Ivar Avenue; 75 percent of the library's ninety thousand volumes were lost, including a huge, irreplaceable, and invaluable collection of early movie scripts, some with annotations by D. W. Griffith. Many other old buildings were also lost to fires both accidental and deliberate. It was really only in the 1990s that effective measures were taken to clean up what many considered to be a sewer. Tourists flocked back—in 1994 there were 9.1 million of them.

In the early 1980s the Hollywood Chamber of Commerce tried to copyright the name "Hollywood," a silly idea which upset many of the people and firms who had been using it for years, while the city of Hollywood in Florida filed a lawsuit to protect its own name! Fortunately, the chamber of commerce of California's Hollywood lost the suit.

Finally, in 2000 the Hollywood Chamber of Commerce woke up to the potential of what little was left of its heritage and set up place markers of famous places on Hollywood Boulevard and Vine Street, indicating the locations of long-vanished sites like the Hollywood Hotel (see chapter 6), the de Longpré house, and the Brown Derby (see chapter 3). But alas, it was too little, too late.

In the next chapters, therefore, we shall take a close look at what little is left of the Golden Age of Hollywood: the few monuments, the studios and theaters, the film sets, the houses and hotels, the cult centers, and above all the graves of the stars.

THREE

Riddle of the Sands
Hollywood Egyptology

It may come as a surprise to learn that there is real archaeology being done in connection with Hollywood. Archaeology is popularly associated with remote periods, but there is no reason why this should be so. As I've noted, the subject concerns all material traces of the human past, from its beginnings up until yesterday. In many parts of the world there has arisen the study of industrial archaeology, investigating and preserving the remains of the machinery of recent times. And since the movie business was certainly an important industry—as well as a major new art form—of the twentieth century, it follows that we should try to study and save what little remains of its embryonic phase. It is already too late for much of it—as we shall see in other chapters, nearly all the old studios have gone, having been torn down for development or, even more tragically, turned into parking lots. In its overwhelming urge to explore the new and to move forward, Hollywood has lost sight of its origins. Even today, very few of the principal sites and monuments from the early days bear plaques to indicate their seminal role.

Yet there is one project afoot to rectify this situation a little, and it concerns Hollywood's view of Egypt. Thanks in large measure to the discovery of Tutankhamen's tomb in 1922, early Hollywood fell in love with ancient Egypt. The most striking example is Sid Grauman's imposing Egyptian Theatre, built in 1922 at 6708 Hollywood Boulevard. The Egyptian Theatre still stands—it had originally been planned as a Spanish- or Moorish-style building, but the Tutankhamen craze swept that idea aside, and instead it became "a temple of art." Its ornate wall decoration is partly based on a scene from the Akh-Menou of Tuthmosis III at Karnak, probably copied from a plate in the classic volume by Karl Lepsius. It was the site of the first gala movie premiere, that of Allan Dwan's *Robin Hood* (starring Douglas Fairbanks) in 1922. The female ushers were dressed as Cleopatras, while men dressed as Egyptian sentries patrolled the parapet. Before the movie began, an orchestra played the overture from Verdi's *Aida*! In 1924 the Egyptian Theatre was likewise the scene of the premiere of Raoul Walsh's *The Thief of Bagdad* (also starring Fairbanks), and in 1926 it hosted a double premiere of William Beaudine's *Sparrows* (starring Mary Pickford) and Albert Parker's *The Black Pirate* (Douglas Fairbanks again). For many years, the Hollywood Egyptian was the best-known movie theater in the United States, and it was considered the "queen of silent movie palaces." It was also the place where the first sound movie, Alan Crosland's *Don Juan* (starring John Barrymore and Mary Astor), was screened in Hollywood in 1925. This film was actually a silent film with music played in sync on records.

Grauman's Egyptian Theatre declined greatly, unlike his Chinese Theatre at 6925 Hollywood Boulevard, eventually being occupied by squatters who were evicted just before a 1974

Grauman's Egyptian Theatre, circa 1927.

earthquake created forty-by-twenty-foot holes in its hollow clay walls. But it was restored to much of its former glory in the late 1990s.

For some reason the Vista Theatre, located at 4473 Sunset Drive, on the very site where in 1914 D. W. Griffith filmed much of his *Birth of a Nation* (the film which made him a millionaire) and *Intolerance*, has an Egyptian-style forecourt, with a ticket booth that seems to have been inspired by the large gilded-wood carrying shrine of the statue of Anubis in Tutankhamen's tomb, along with other finds from the same source. The hieroglyphs and cartouches bear the name of Tutankhamen and of divinities, albeit somewhat inaccurately copied. As with the Grauman building, it is said that the theater's owners had begun to build it in Spanish style, but then they switched to Egyptian decor on hearing of the discovery of King Tut's tomb in 1922. It opened in 1923 with a mixed bill of vaudeville acts and silent movies.

However, a far bigger Egyptian monument remains, 170 miles north of Los Angeles, at Guadalupe.

The Egyptian foyer of the Vista Theatre—Note the handprints and footprints in the foreground.

Here the coastal sand dunes had served as the Arabian Desert in George Melford's *The Sheik* (1921), starring Rudolph Valentino, and would later do so again in George Fitzmaurice's *Son of the Sheik* (1926), also starring Valentino. They also became North Africa in Josef von Sternberg's *Morocco* (1930), which starred Marlene Dietrich, and colonial Iraq in Louis Gasnier and Charles Barton's *The Last Outpost* (1935), starring Cary Grant. In 1922–1923, Cecil B. DeMille directed part of his first silent version of *The Ten Commandments* here, at a cost of $1.4 million. It was this film which began his subsequent reputation for huge epics with gargantuan sets. It was also a pioneer production in many other ways through its extraordinary special effects, such as the pillar of fire and the parting of the Red Sea, and its early use of Technicolor. Moses was played by Theodore Roberts, Miriam by Estelle Taylor, and Rameses by Charles DeRoche.

Paramount Studios had told DeMille that it was too expensive to film in Egypt, so instead, out in the sand dunes near Guadalupe, he constructed the City of Rameses on a stunning and unprecedented scale in movie history. The statistics are staggering: 1,000 construction workers and craftsmen (some accounts claim 1,500–1,600) toiled day and night for a month, with over half a million feet of timber, 30 tons of plaster, 25,000 pounds of nails, and 75 miles of reinforcing cable and bracing wire. The city walls, 720 feet wide and 10 stories (120 feet) high, were decorated with a 70-foot-high bas-relief in plaster, depicting two archers in horse-drawn chariots. In front, copied from the originals at Abu Simbel, were four statues of the seated Rameses II flanking the gate—each was 35 feet high and weighed 39 tons. Leading to the city's entrance was an avenue 1,000 feet wide and lined with twenty-one big-bosomed sphinxes—made of concrete, they weighed over 4 tons apiece. The statuary weighed a total of 1 million pounds. All of this was shipped by train from Hollywood to Guadalupe—the sphinxes in pieces, as they were so big.

Filming involved 2,500–3,000 extras, as well as some 250 soldiers and 7 officers from the 11th Cavalry and the 76th Field Artillery to act as charioteers for the 300 specially built chariots. Food was provided by 125 cooks, and water was kept plentiful by two giant pumps which constantly raised 100 gallons per minute, filling four tanks of 18,000 gallons each. Cast and crew lived for twelve weeks in what became known as "Camp DeMille"—a tent city (complete with hospital) just out of camera shot for 3,000 men, women, and children, as well as for 4,000–5,000 animals from farms and zoos around the county which were needed for

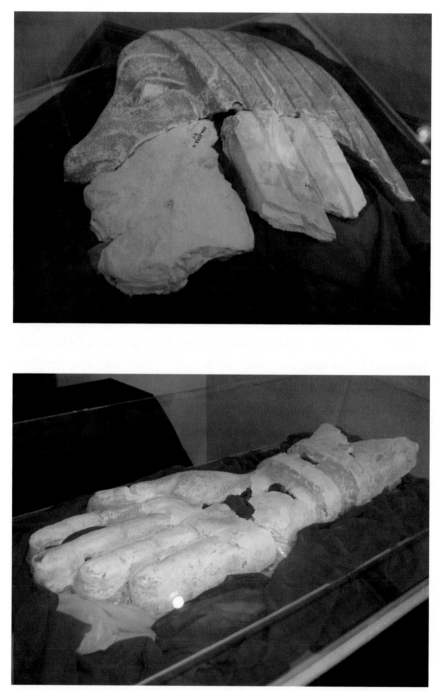

Huge fragments of plaster reliefs from the Guadalupe site—head and hand.

the exodus scene. The amazing logistics of providing for the humans alone can be seen in the requirements for a single lunch: 7,500 sandwiches, 2,500 pieces of fruit, and 400 gallons of coffee! Kosher meals had to be trucked in for the several hundred Orthodox Jews hired as extras. The giant mess tent could seat 1,500 people. Moreover, the animals required 20,000 pounds of hay per day. When running costs escalated to $40,000 a day, the panic-stricken studio sent telegrams, to which DeMille responded, "What do they want me to do? Stop now and release it as *The Five Commandments*?" By the end of production, the film had cost $1.4 million, as mentioned above, but fortunately it grossed more than $4 million. Its premiere, appropriately enough, took place at Grauman's Egyptian Theatre on December 4, 1923.

After filming was finished, DeMille ordered the set to be partly dismantled and buried. The city walls were chopped off and toppled backward: a three-hundred-foot-long trench was dug, and a horse-drawn bulldozer toppled the edifice into it. Much of the set remains there, beneath the sand, and thus it affords a unique opportunity to the archaeologist of film history. Other huge sets were constructed during those pioneer days, as we shall see—Griffith's Babylon, Fairbanks's Nottingham Castle, and the Colosseum built in the Malibu Mountains for Fred Niblo's silent *Ben-Hur*; all are now gone. DeMille's own City of Jerusalem, built for his 1927 *King of Kings*, survived a while, only to serve as the blazing Atlanta in *Gone with the Wind*—the first scene to be filmed, in order to clear the set. In an industry where sets are temporary phenomena—redundant obstructions once a scene has been filmed—it is inevitable, if regrettable, that few have survived. A fire at Universal studios in 1990 destroyed some venerable sets, and many of MGM's back-lot backdrops have been replaced by office buildings. The "teardown" mentality is not limited to houses and studios.

But DeMille's Egyptian set still exists, the only one to do so from those early days, and it is vital to preserve it. In 1985, archaeologists from the University of California at Santa Barbara made a preliminary examination of the site: the head of one of the horses from the great plaster bas-relief had already been uncovered so the approximate layout of the set beneath the dune could be worked out. It was decided to proceed with a magnetometer survey by which to determine the exact extent of the foundations and walls. Ground-penetrating radar has subsequently located what remains beneath the sand (about a third has already been destroyed by the elements), and pieces of wood, plaster, metal and glass have been plotted. Excavation is difficult in the wet sand as special chemicals are needed to soak the plaster and harden it.

The dunes, now an official State of California registered and protected archaeological site, are managed by the Nature Conservancy, which protects the snowy plovers which nest in the sand from mid-March to September. The conservancy has permitted a series of limited digs to take place in recent years, although, despite decades of appeals and financial and bureaucratic problems are still causing delays to major excavation. For the actual digging, spades are not much required: trowels and brushes are more appropriate, and perhaps even the type of blower used by gardeners in Beverly Hills to remove dead leaves from lawns. The sand is loose—and indeed, protection from the fierce winds is necessary to keep the workers from being sandblasted and to prevent each day's work from being covered again by morning. It is also necessary to work fast since word quickly gets around, and souvenir hunters are often on the prowl. But a number of finds are already on show at the Dunes Center in Guadalupe, while others are still being treated in preparation for display.

Among the finds are everyday items, most notably glass bottles for milk and cough medicine. As the film was shot during the Prohibition era, it is thought that many people found a way around the law by drinking brands of cough syrup that contained up to 12 percent alcohol! There are also pseudo-Roman coins which DeMille gave as souvenirs to extras on the film—on one side they have a helmeted Roman soldier's head in profile, with 45 BC underneath!

It is known that DeMille was afraid that if he left the set standing, rival filmmakers would come to Guadalupe and shoot movies on the cheap, movies that might even appear before his own. But the question still remains: Why on earth did he decide to bury it rather than dismantle it completely? One possibility is that having overspent on production, he could not afford the

The mock-Roman coins given out by DeMille.

expense of a careful recovery of materials or a full demolition and removal. But it seems more likely that he had a romantic notion that the set should be preserved for a future resurrection of this type; indeed, in his posthumously published autobiography, one can sense his amusement at the possibility:

> If 1,000 years from now archaeologists happen to dig beneath the sands of Guadalupe, I hope they will not rush into print with the amazing news that Egyptian civilization, far from being confined to the valley of the Nile, extended all the way to the Pacific Coast of North America. The sphinxes they will find were buried there when we had finished with them and dismantled our huge set of the gates of Pharaoh's city.

If this excavation project is ever carried to a successful conclusion, then we shall at last have a fitting monument to the pioneer days of Hollywood. Somewhat ironically, the Guadalupe site has itself become the subject of a fictional movie, *Sands of Oblivion* (2007), in which an archaeologist couple and an Iraq War veteran uncover "the secret that DeMille could not keep hidden" and "unleash a horror that cannot be stopped." According to the plot, DeMille destroyed the set as a ploy to hide the fact that he had entrapped the evil god Im-La-Ra on one of the stages, using an ancient curse. And of course the archaeologists investigating the site unwittingly release the evil god . . .

As a final postscript, it is worth mentioning that the two fake stone tablets brandished by Charlton Heston in DeMille's color *Ten Commandments* of 1956 were displayed for many years inside the Episcopal Church of St. Stephen, just off Hollywood Boulevard at 6128 Yucca—the very church which was attended by DeMille and his family and where his funeral took place in 1959. They were twenty-three inches tall, twelve inches wide, and they were made of fiberglass on a wood backing, with an early Canaanite script on them. However, they were removed by the DeMille Foundation a few years ago, and in December 2012 they were sold at an auction of film memorabilia. According to the auction brochure, they were made to look irregular and chipped, having been "carved" by divine fire. The work of Paramount Studios' scenic artist A. J. Ciraolo, the tablets were carefully painted to resemble carved stone. The successful bidder, who paid $60,000, was unnamed, so we don't know who took the tablets!

FOUR

The Industrial Zone

The Industrialization of Dreams

In this and following chapters, I look at the sad neglect of Hollywood history, despite the global importance and influence of the products made there. The movie business never had much of a sense of history about itself, and a huge amount of material has been destroyed, as in any archaeological culture. But archaeology's specialty is piecing together the past from the disparate fragments left behind when most clues have disappeared.

When Paramount moved its archives some years ago, it burned most of the material they contained, an entire warehouse filled wall to wall and floor to ceiling with filing cabinets and bookshelves. Many films have also been destroyed: in the early 1960s, silent films were thought to have no commercial value; in addition, they were difficult to store, dangerous to handle, and a fire hazard. Some were burned in studio fires; others had simply disintegrated by the 1950s or were in such a bad condition that they were taken out of the vaults, cut into small pieces with a chain saw, and burned to salvage the silver content of the film stock.

This chapter covers the "activity areas" and specialized structures where the original work of Hollywood was done: the remains of the sites of the first studios, many of them now parking lots; the locations of some magnificent sets; and the movie theaters where the products of the "Hollywood Culture" were displayed to its people.

CORN FACTORIES AND SCHMALTZ MINES: THE STUDIOS

The early major studios were run almost as feudal kingdoms, ruled with an iron hand by men who were mostly recent immigrants. These future moguls began as glove salesmen, furriers, pool hustlers, garbagemen. . . . They jumped into the untested waters of the movie business, creating a product that crossed all barriers of class, race, and language. Their power grew so great that Stalin declared that if he could only control the film industry, he could control the world.

As we saw in chapter 2, the New York Biograph Company had been sending units to southern California every winter since 1906, while the first permanent Los Angeles movie studio was created by the Selig-Polyscope Company. It was located at 751 South Olive, and was opened in 1909 by a film producer named William Selig. He came to Los Angeles from New York and rented an old mansion on this site, where he shot the first film to be made entirely in California. In addition, he also built the first Hollywood motion picture set in the backyard—the film was called *In the Sultan's Power*. The site is, inevitably, a parking area now, without even a plaque.

Hollywood's first studio (at 6101–6121 Sunset Boulevard) was built in 1911 when the producers Al Christie and David Horsley of the Nestor Film Company rented a tavern and barn on the northwest corner of Sunset and Gower—the site is now a parking lot. In 1912 this studio merged with Universal Studios, and the site became Christie Studios, where comedies were made. It is now CBS. In 1911, Christie filmed one of Hollywood's first movies, a comedy short, in the orange groves just to the north of this site. He later bought the groves, and in 1925 he built the Regent Hotel (later called the Hastings) on the very spot where this comedy was shot.

The Nestor Film Company was not the only arrival in 1911—there was also the New York Motion Picture Corporation. Indeed, within three months of Nestor's arrival in town, fifteen more film companies had arrived, renting land along Sunset Boulevard, where it was cheaper than along Hollywood Boulevard. All four corners of Gower and Sunset were rapidly occupied by companies making a stream of comedies, Westerns, and melodramas. By 1912, Vitagraph, Kalem, Edison, Universal, and Lubin all had studios in the area. Vitagraph bought twenty-nine acres of sheep pasture at the eastern end of Prospect Avenue and built an extensive studio there.

Century Movie Studios (6100 Sunset), owned by Universal Studios in 1912, later turned into the L-Ko Comedy studio, and in 1918 it was named Century Studios. The site is now a shopping center.

So by late 1913, when Cecil B. DeMille hit town, Los Angeles was already a major center for movie production. What brought this future giant of the "Hollywood Culture" here?

Jesse Lasky was a theatrical and vaudeville producer in New York who met and befriended Cecil Blount DeMille, who was an actor-writer-director. Together they wrote and produced a successful play called *California*. But DeMille had grown bored and was seeking a new adventure—he was thirty-two years old with a wife and daughter to support and a mountain of debts after years in the theater. Lasky's brother-in-law Samuel Goldwyn (originally Goldfish) was a glove salesman, and he had recently suggested that the new moviemaking business might be lucrative. And that is why—to protect DeMille from finding a foolhardy way out of his financial woes—Lasky and Goldwyn joined with him to found the Jesse L. Lasky Feature Play Company in 1913.

They bought the rights to a 1902 play, *The Squaw Man* by Edwin Milton Royle, and drew up plans to film it in Arizona. As a Western, most of its action could be shot outdoors, thus cutting down on lighting costs. But when DeMille and his team reached Flagstaff, it was raining and there were two feet of snow on the ground. Even worse, there were high mountains around, and the movie required plains. So they proceeded to Los Angeles and took up residence in the Alexandria Hotel, which was located downtown near the financial district.

In 1912, Harry Revier and L. L. Burns had rented a horse barn in Hollywood from businessman Jacob Stern to use as offices, dressing rooms, and a film laboratory. They also built an outdoor stage next to it and began to rent this to new film companies (in that same year Warner Brothers, Universal, and Fox were all founded). It was soon recognized as one of the best-equipped rental lots in Hollywood. DeMille was looking for a suitable place to do his filming, and when Revier and Burns heard this, they drove him out to Hollywood to show him their facility. Since he found the barn acceptable, it was sublet to him for $250 per month (some sources claim $75), and it was agreed that the laboratory would develop the film and that a second stage would be built on the property solely for the use of the

Lasky Company. Within two years, the barn was purchased by the company as its permanent studio.

The original site of what became known as the Famous Players–Lasky studio was at 1521 Vine (at the corner of Selma and Vine)—and this is where Jesse Lasky and Cecil B. DeMille made *The Squaw Man*, Hollywood's first "feature-length" picture. The shoot took eighteen days, beginning on December 29, 1913. The movie cost $15,450, was released on February 23, 1914, and it made the producers a profit of $244,700.

The studio's original site is now the Hollywood Palladium, a bank and a huge parking lot, but mercifully the Lasky-DeMille Barn itself (where Rudolph Valentino was to make most of his films) was moved in 1926 to Paramount Studios—where it was renovated and repainted to serve as a rehearsal hall—and then to its present site at 2100 Highland, opposite the Hollywood Bowl, where it survives as the Hollywood Heritage Museum (or Hollywood Studio Museum). A plaque on the outside calls it "Hollywood's First Major Film Company Studio" and states that half of the structure, then in use as a barn, was rented by DeMille as the studio where he would make *The Squaw Man*. Another plaque inside proclaims it as "The Birthplace of Paramount Studio."

Today the interior of the barn contains a facsimile of DeMille's office around 1914, complete with his hat, shoes, and puttees; a wealth of exhibits from the silent era, such as sandals worn in the silent *Ben-Hur*, and a spear from the silent *Ten Commandments* (see chapter 3) as well as props from the later color version; a vast range of Valentino memorabilia; a movie camera from Charlie Chaplin's studio; a 1916 Cameragraph Projector; and two enormous projectors used by Buster Keaton for showing movies at home.

The corner of Sunset and Gower (at 6098 Sunset), during the late teens and early 1920s, was where many "movie

Charlie Chaplin camera at the Lasky-DeMille Barn.

cowboys" would hang around—often in costume—in the hope of being hired for bit parts or as extras in the Westerns being made in the small studios in that area. So the corner was nicknamed "Gower Gulch," while the area nearby was called Poverty Row

Keaton projectors at the Lasky-DeMille Barn.

because of the numerous small, struggling studios there which scraped by through making one- and two-reel Westerns and comedies—one of these (at 1438 Gower) was Columbia Studios, founded by Harry Cohn in 1921. Gower Gulch is now a

Gower Gulch as it looks today.

small parking lot with shops on two sides, but it has retained the name, and the shopping plaza built in 1976 has been designed to look like a back-lot Western street with boardwalks and suitable facades.

The Jasper Studio was built in 1919 (at 1040 Las Palmas Avenue). This is where Howard Hughes made *Hell's Angels* in 1927 and where Jean Harlow made her debut in the movies. It later became known as the Metropolitan (in the 1920s), Educational Studios (in 1931), Hollywood General Studios (in 1947)—and Francis Ford Coppola's Zoetrope Studios (in 1980).

The Metro, which has become known as Hollywood's "Phantom" Studio (at 6300 Romaine), was built before 1920 and was then the biggest in town, covering five city blocks. This is where Valentino shot *The Four Horsemen of the Apocalypse* in

1921, the film which made his name. But when Metro merged with the Goldwyn studios in 1924 to become Metro-Goldwyn-Mayer (MGM) the Metro site was abandoned, sold, and then destroyed. Part of the site is now a huge parking lot.

Yet another lost studio is the Lone Star (at 1025 Lillian Way) where Charlie Chaplin made his wonderful first films in 1916–1917 (*The Immigrant*, *The Floorwalker*, *Easy Street*) and where Buster Keaton also made films in the 1920s. It is now—surprise, surprise—a parking lot.

L. Frank Baum, author of *The Wonderful Wizard of Oz* (1899), moved to Hollywood in 1911 and built a house, "Ozcot," on the southwest corner of Cherokee Avenue and Yucca Street, one block north of Hollywood Boulevard. Eventually he decided to enter the burgeoning movie business as he realized that films were taking away the audience from his theatrical productions. His firm, the Oz Film Manufacturing Company, was established on the northwest corner of Santa Monica and

The Warner Brothers Studio on Sunset Boulevard (postcard).

Gower, and in 1914 it made its first movie, *The Patchwork Girl of Oz*. Unfortunately, there was no market for Baum's films, which were dismissed as "kids' stuff," and so he retired to Ozcot with wounded pride. The house was demolished in 1953 to make way for an apartment block.

Carl Laemmle came to California from New York in 1912, and in 1914 he created Universal Studios on the site of a 230-acre chicken ranch at Lankershim in the North Hollywood foothills. It was the first studio to realize the advantages of allowing the public to visit and tour—busloads of tourists were brought from Los Angeles to see how movies were made. For 25 cents they could stand on observation platforms and watch scenes being shot. By 1917 it was decided that the tourists were something of a nuisance, and the practice was stopped; but in the late 1950s, at a time of a serious slump in the industry, Universal once again pioneered the studio tour, charging for admission, and earning a fortune in the process. It now has millions of visitors every year.

At 5858 Sunset Boulevard is an elegant neo-colonial building built in 1918 by four brothers by the name of Warner. This is where they eventually revolutionized the movie industry by perfecting synchronized sound. In 1929 Warner Brothers moved its headquarters to Burbank, and the building on Sunset was used for the production of the legendary Looney Tunes cartoons starring Bugs Bunny, Daffy Duck, and many other wonderful characters. In 1942 the building was acquired by Paramount, and it later became a huge bowling center. Currently it is Sunset Bronson Studios.

The RKO studios (short for Radio-Keith-Orpheum) were built in 1920–1921 at 780 Gower Street (the corner with Melrose Avenue), starting life as Robertson-Cole Studios, becoming then FBO Studios (1923; owned by Joseph Kennedy, father of John F. Kennedy) and finally RKO in 1928. It was bought by

The famous Paramount gate on Melrose.

Howard Hughes in 1948. Each RKO movie began with the image of a huge globe with a radio tower on top of it, and lightning bolts that spelled out "RKO-Radio Pictures." RKO now forms part of Paramount Studios, but its iconic globe can still be seen on the soundstage's roof.

Paramount itself stands on one of the oldest studio lots in Hollywood (at 5451 Marathon Street), which was built in

The MGM Studio entrance as it was in 1928. (Courtesy of hollywoodphotosgraphs .com.)

1917–1918 as Peralta Studios, becoming then Brunton Studios (1920), United Studios (1921–1926), and finally Paramount. It still features one of the last great icons of old Hollywood, the famous wrought-iron side gate on Marathon, which featured so memorably in Billy Wilder's *Sunset Boulevard*, when Erich von Stroheim drove Gloria Swanson through it in her magnificent Isotta-Fraschini car. It has lost its superstructure over the years, but it remains a beautiful and magical sight, a fragment of a Golden Age.

In 1917 William Fox, a former street peddler, bought thirteen acres of land on both sides of Western Avenue at Sunset (1417–1418 North Western) and constructed Fox Studios, where stars such as Tom Mix and Theda Bara (the "Vamp") made many movies, and where John Wayne made his first film in 1928. Fox merged with Twentieth Century Pictures in 1935, and production moved to the Beverly Hills area. Once again, the original Fox lot was torn down in the 1960s and replaced by stores and parking lots.

MGM Studios were originally called Triangle Studios, and were built in 1915 by D. W. Griffith, Mack Sennett, and Thomas H. Ince. In 1918, MGM Studios became Sam Goldwyn Studios, and in 1924, after the three studios merged, Metro-Goldwyn-Mayer. The grandiose entrance still survives at 10202 West Washington Boulevard.

Part of Mack Sennett's "Keystone Kops" studio at 1712 Glendale Boulevard still survives, miraculously—it was originally the Bison studios in 1909, but Sennett bought it in 1912 and called it Keystone. This is where, in 1913, the first custard pie was thrown in a movie—by Mabel Normand at Ben Turpin.

The surviving Mack Sennett soundstage.

Many of the greats began their careers here, including Charlie Chaplin, Roscoe Arbuckle, and Gloria Swanson. Sennett left the twenty-eight-acre studio in 1928, but one soundstage remains. It looks like a big white warehouse and was used for a while as a scene and costume shop for the Center Theater Group, but it now appears to be a storage depot.

Charlie Chaplin built his own studio in 1918 at 1416 La Brea, in pseudo-Tudor style. He bought the land for $35,000, and sold it in 1953 for $650,000. There was some opposition to his placing a studio here amid lovely homes, and so he placated the locals by erecting a quaint facade resembling a row of English houses. Here he made *A Dog's Life* (1918), *The Kid* (1920), *The Gold Rush* (1925), *City Lights* (1931), *Modern Times* (1936), *The Great Dictator* (1940), and others. Much later, for many years, it was the home of Herb Alpert's A&M Records, and since 1999 it has been owned by Jim Henson Studios. The inner courtyard is little changed. It contains Chaplin's footprints in cement and also a large metal door in a wall which leads to the safe in which he kept his footage. Not far away, at 1328–1330 North Formosa Avenue, is an apartment court of unusually shaped bungalows resembling a French village, with a narrow street of

The Chaplin studio on La Brea.

The Robin Hood set at the Pickford-Fairbanks Studio (postcard, above), and "The Lot" on the site today (below).

cobblestones. This was allegedly built around 1920 by Chaplin as a movie set, and it is said that Valentino once lived here.

Farther down Formosa, at 1041, on the southwest corner of Santa Monica and Formosa, is the site of what in 1920 was Hampton Studios, which was bought in 1922 by Mary Pickford and Douglas Fairbanks and renamed Pickford-Fairbanks Studio. This is where the giant castle set was built for Fairbanks's *Robin Hood* (1922). In 1927 Sam Goldwyn became their partner, and it became the Goldwyn Studios. He became the sole owner in 1949. Today it is a building known as "The Lot."

In 1925 Walt Disney and his brother Roy had their small first studio in a tiny store at 4649 Kingswell Avenue. Walt had arrived in Hollywood in 1923 and boarded with his uncle Robert at 4406 Kingswell. Here, in a small garage behind the house, he made his first Hollywood cartoon film, *Alice's Wonderland*. In 1981 the ga-

The plaque marking the site of the Disney studio where a grocery now stands.

rage was bought by a local historical society and removed. Disney built his second studio—a fine, white Spanish colonial edifice—at 2719 Hyperion Avenue in 1926, and he made the first Mickey Mouse cartoon, *Plane Crazy*, there, and numerous others, culminating in *Snow White and the Seven Dwarfs* in 1937. He moved operations in 1940 to 500 South Buena Vista in Burbank, and this historic studio has been torn down. It is now a huge Gelson's Market, and only a small plaque on a streetlight outside identifies this "Point of Historical Interest."

The present Disney Studios have a mouse-head motif along the top of their metal railings, and wonderful caryatids of the Seven Dwarfs holding up the roof on the main building's facade. How would an archaeologist of the future interpret these figures?

Howard Hughes moved into his former headquarters (at 7000–7010 Romaine Street) in 1927, and this is where films

The dwarf caryatids (far right) and mouse-theme fence at today's Disney Studios.

Howard Hughes's former headquarters.

such as *Hell's Angels* (1930), *Scarface* (1932), and *The Outlaw* (1943) were edited. Today it is a "Producers Film Center," a climate-controlled building for film and tape security storage.

Culver City became a center for moviemaking simply because in 1915 a real estate developer offered free land in this shabby suburb to anyone willing to build a motion picture studio on it. The first to take up the offer was Thomas H. Ince, followed by Sam Goldwyn and Hal Roach. Culver Studios, at 9336 West Washington Boulevard, was built in 1918 by Ince, and had many changes of name—Pathé in 1924; DeMille in 1925 (his *King of Kings* was filmed here in 1927); RKO-Pathé in 1931 (*King Kong* was made here in 1933); but in 1935 it became the Selznick studio, the period of its greatest fame when *Gone with the Wind* was shot (1939). Later *Citizen Kane* (1941) was also shot here. The main building, a neo-colonial white mansion said to be based on George Washington's home at Mount Vernon, appears at the beginning of all Selznick's movies, including *Gone with the Wind*, and part of its facade was also used as a southern mansion in that film.

Hal Roach Studios, home of all the classic Laurel and Hardy comedies, as well as early Harold Lloyd films and some serious films such as Lewis Milestone's *Of Mice and Men* (1939), was at 8222 West Washington Boulevard. There is now a tiny green area on a street corner here with a picnic table, two benches, and a plaque which says, "Site of the Hal Roach Studios . . . Laugh factory to the World . . . 1919–1963." Sadly this is all that now remains of one of the greatest factories of the "Hollywood Culture."

The old Selznick studio, now Culver Studios.

Hal Roach Studios (postcard), now demolished.

Plaque marking the site of now-demolished Hal Roach Studios.

PUTTING SKIN ON BALONEY: THE SETS

Movies were first shot on platforms in the open air under big muslin sheets—to diffuse the strong sunlight—so that scenes often looked somewhat windy. Actors were expected to bring their own costumes; workmen brought their own tools. The public were welcome to watch filming, as long as they did not come into the shots—and of course in silent movies noise was no problem, unless it distracted the actors. Some directors even employed musicians to play off-camera to set the mood. Eventually, enclosed stages sprang up, and indoor sets were constructed, in which filming used arc lamps.

As moviemaking became prominent and ubiquitous, the residents of Hollywood grew used to everything from fake bank robberies to people marching down thoroughfares, and streets being roped off or hosed down to cause cars to skid, and endless chases, often involving carloads of comedy cops! Sets were constructed in studios or sometimes far from Hollywood (see chapter 3).

The site of the greatest outdoor movie set ever built—the enormous Babylon set for D. W. Griffith's *Intolerance*—was erected in 1915 at 4500 Sunset Boulevard (at the intersection with Virgil Avenue), on a lot known as Majestic-Reliance Studios (later it became the Fine Arts Studio in the 1920s, and Talisman Studios in the 1930s). The set was supposed to represent part of Belshazzar's palace of the third millennium BC, with numerous giant carvings rendered in plaster by Italian craftsmen. Indeed, Griffith was heavily influenced by the Italian director Giovanni Pastrone, whose film *Cabiria* was made in 1913. *Cabiria* was about Carthage being besieged by Romans, and hence the movie had elephants in its decor. This is presumably why Griffith insisted on likewise having giant elephant sculptures on his set, even though these animals are not known ever to have set foot in Babylon! What one cannot see in the footage or the stills is that the set was a highly colorful construction. Due to its vast size—the towers were 200 feet high, the elephants 30 feet high, and the walls 90 feet high and 150 feet long—it dominated the intersection, but it was also vulnerable. It had to be lashed down during Santa Ana windstorms; and when it was filled with the 3,500 people required for the scene—dancing girls parading down the great staircase, onlookers on the many platforms, soldiers and horses on the high walls—it almost collapsed under the tremendous weight. It is said that *Intolerance* cost about $1.9 million to make—the costliest movie up to that time—though

The Babylon set from Griffith's Intolerance. *(Courtesy of hollywoodphotographs. com.)*

others have claimed it cost a mere $285,000. Be that as it may, it is clear that a good percentage of the money must have been spent on the Babylon sequence.

Unfortunately the movie was a flop, as audiences did not care for Griffith's moral lessons. Hounded by investors, he headed for England to shoot footage for his next film, *Hearts of the World*; and on his return to Hollywood, he built war sets for that film amid the walls of Babylon. The vast set gradually fell into ruins over the years and—at Griffith's own suggestion—became a tourist attraction, but it was also used as a playground by local children. It was this decaying set which gave rise to the now-clichéd nickname "Hollywood Babylon." In 1919 there was some talk of it being preserved as a permanent landmark, but, as

The new version of part of the Babylon set, on Hollywood Boulevard, with a view of the Hollywood sign beyond.

so often in Hollywood, nothing came of it. By the end of 1922, the land had been sold for $100,000, and the set was replaced by housing and the 900-seat Bard's Playhouse, now the Vista Theatre.

Absolutely nothing remains of the set or the studio today—stores and parking lots cover the area. In recent years, a modern version of part of the Babylonian set, together with a few elephant statues, has been built in a shopping mall on Hollywood Boulevard, just east of the Chinese Theatre, on the site of the Hollywood Hotel, and with a view of the Hollywood sign. At long last, therefore, some homage has been paid to that extraordinary, vast, 1915 set.

But a few places where famous old movies were shot do survive despite the passing of the years. In *A Perfect Day* (1929), Laurel and Hardy were parked with guests in front of a house located at 3120 Vera Avenue in Culver City, endlessly attempting and failing to drive off for a picnic. The house still stands, unchanged. Similarly, in *Big Business* (1929), one of their last silent films, they try in vain to sell a Christmas tree to James Finlayson, and in the steadily rising conflict he demolishes their car as they tear his house apart. This house too, at 10281 Dunleer Drive, Los Angeles, remains unchanged. According to Hal Roach, the wrong house was destroyed—its owners were away, and returned as the destruction was going on! Finally, at 929 Vendome Street, Silverlake, one can still climb the iconic 131-step staircase up which, in the Academy Award–winning film *The Music Box* (1932), Laurel and Hardy struggled to deliver a player piano to a house at the top. They also filmed here for *Hats Off* (1927), in which they were delivering a washing machine—a silent film which is missing and actively being hunted by the "Silent Comedy Mafia." Only stills survive. But the stairway, one of the most precious survivals of the Golden Age, has barely changed.

Still from Laurel and Hardy's A Perfect Day, *from the author's collection.*

The house in Laurel and Hardy's A Perfect Day.

Still from Laurel and Hardy's Big Business, *from the author's collection.*

The house in Laurel and Hardy's Big Business.

In these three places, for once, it is as if time in Hollywood has stood still. It is sad that so few such features survive. For example, Culver City Hall, a beautiful Beaux-Arts building at 9770 Culver Boulevard, appeared as a hospital in Laurel and Hardy's *County Hospital* (1932) and as a courthouse in their *Going Bye-Bye!* (1934)—but it has now been replaced by a modern building.

INFLATED SHADOWS—AND EGOS—ON A SCREEN: THE MOVIE THEATERS

Ironically, Hollywood did not get its first movie theater until quite late, in 1910 or early 1911, thus lagging behind the rest of the country. Known as The Idyl Hour, it was located on the northeast corner of Hollywood Boulevard (6525) and Hudson. It consisted of a small wooden building—a converted store—with a screen, a projector, and some chairs and benches. Three years later it was renamed The Iris, perhaps because Hollywood's serious and God-fearing citizens did not approve of idleness! Having first moved to 6415 Hollywood Boulevard in 1914, four years later it moved to a much grander building, containing a thousand seats, at 6508 Hollywood Boulevard and Wilcox Avenue. Walt Disney used The Iris to preview some of his early cartoons, as well as the Vista Theatre.

At 307 South Broadway in Los Angeles is the Million Dollar Theater built for Sid Grauman in 1917, its extreme baroque style featuring gargoyles and Moorish carvings. It opened with a screening of *The Silent Man*, starring cowboy actor William S. Hart.

As mentioned in chapter 3, the Egyptian Theatre (at 6708 Hollywood Boulevard) held the very first movie premiere—that of Douglas Fairbanks's *Robin Hood* in 1922.

Still from Laurel and Hardy's The Music Box, *from the author's collection.*

The Orpheum is the best preserved movie theater in Los Angeles, at 842 South Broadway; it opened in 1926 and has oak paneling, Gothic arches, art-deco furniture, and a ceiling of gold leaf. The El Capitan (at 6838 Hollywood Boulevard) was also opened in 1926, as a legitimate live theater, with a stage 120 feet wide. The lavish building was considered one of the most palatial structures in America. It was subsequently adapted for movies and renamed the Paramount Theatre, and it held the premiere of *Citizen Kane* in May 1941. In recent years it was acquired by Disney, which gave it a $40 million facelift, restored the name "El Capitan," and now uses it as a showcase for its animated features.

Very close to the El Capitan, but on the opposite side of the road, stands Mann's (Grauman's) Chinese Theatre (at 6925

The staircase in Laurel and Hardy's Hats Off *and* The Music Box.

Hollywood Boulevard). Francis X. Bushman's house had stood on this site, but it was demolished, and in November 1925 the actress Anna May Wong drove in the first rivet for the theater. The new building opened in May 1927 with the premiere of

The revamped El Capitan theater today. (Courtesy of the Library of Congress, Prints and Photographs Division, photograph by Carol M. Highsmith [LC-IG-highsm-04927].)

Cecil B. DeMille's silent film *The King of Kings*. This pseudo-Chinese temple rapidly became the most famous movie theater in the world, a veritable shrine to film. It was scented with sandalwood and had a huge Wurlitzer organ, with an enormous stage which Sid Grauman used for lavish shows. For example, for the opening of Charlie Chaplin's *The Circus* in 1928, a circus appeared on the stage, complete with a Chaplin look-alike; and after the end of George Fitzmaurice's *Mata Hari* (1931), starring Greta Garbo, seventy-five girls dressed in Louis XVI costumes descended five staircases and disappeared into a pool to perform an underwater ballet! They resurfaced in iridescent costumes and wearing headdresses that sprayed water, while fountains on the staircases also sprayed, ballerinas waved multicolored fans of ostrich feathers, and the whole thing was lit by

The Chinese Theatre today. Mann's (formerly Grauman's) Chinese Theatre is the ultimate Hollywood tourist attraction, with crowds often jamming the patio to inspect handprints of movie stars. The opening of Grauman's in 1927 was the most spectacular theater opening in film history. (Courtesy of the Library of Congress, Prints and Photographs Division, photograph by Carol M. Highsmith [LC-HS503-489].)

spotlights of different colors. This does not usually happen in movie theaters today! In the 1940s this was also the venue for the Academy Awards ceremony. Over the years, the Chinese Theatre has held more movie premieres than any other theater—for example, for the opening of Victor Fleming's *The Wizard of Oz* in August 1939, a special "Munchkinland" was constructed in the forecourt!

Even today a premiere there remains quite an event. I stood outside the theater to see such an event one evening in 1981, the premiere of a Burt Reynolds movie called *Paternity*—not exactly a blockbuster! But the powerful searchlights piercing the sky were extraordinary, and the subsequent parade of guests down the boulevard on a red carpet was an enjoyable opportunity to do some star spotting, although apart from Fred MacMurray, Art Linkletter, and Cheryl Ladd I did not recognize anyone— this was not really an "A-list event"! I even probably ruined the evening of one actress who had better remain nameless. When this beautiful blonde came past me on the red carpet, I recognized her face from TV shows, so I took a photograph of her. She graciously paused, smiled and said, "Thank you!" I replied, "Thank you. Who are you?" at which her smile abruptly disappeared and she snapped, "Well, you'd better ask somebody else that." Inevitably, as soon as she had moved on, I remembered who she was! I have felt terribly guilty ever since.

What was then the biggest movie theater in Hollywood was built by Warner Brothers in fourteen months starting in late 1926 at Hollywood Boulevard and Wilcox Avenue. This temple of luxury had walnut paneling, beautiful lounges, genuine antiques, a smoking room, a music room, and even a nursery complete with toys! It was also the first movie theater on the west coast to be wired for sound, and it was due to open with Warner's first talkie, *The Jazz Singer*, but the death of Sam

Warner, one of the brothers, the day before that movie's New York premiere, delayed the Hollywood theater's opening by six months. The building was dedicated to his memory. So the first talkie presented in Hollywood, at the Warner Theatre in 1928, was *Glorious Betsy*, featuring Conrad Nagel. It was an electric moment when an actor first spoke during the screening. Warner Brothers had installed an enormous organ in the theater, just in case talking movies were a flop. They need not have worried! The immediate success of talkies transformed Warner Brothers into a major studio.

Even the Warner Theatre was eclipsed in 1930 by the Pantages Theatre, which opened on June 4, 1930, with the Marion Davies film *Floradora Girl*. Located at 6233 Hollywood Boulevard, it was the last and the largest palace of movies to be built in Hollywood, as well as the very first art-deco theater in the whole of North America. It had a huge vaulted lobby, with twin stairways at either end, a vast auditorium, and a stage 70 feet wide and 180 feet long. Had it not been for the stock market crash, it would have been far bigger—up to twelve stories! It was used for the Academy Awards ceremonies throughout the 1950s, the period which saw their debut on television in 1953.

In downtown Los Angeles, at 1044 South Hill Street, is the Mayan Theater. Originally a theater for plays, it opened in 1927 with Anita Loos's *Gentlemen Prefer Blondes*. Later it became a high-class burlesque house in which legend has it that Marilyn Monroe once worked as a stripper, using the names Marilyn Marlowe and Mona Monroe. The fantastic decoration of the facade is clearly Mayan in inspiration, but it is also a pastiche of Zapotec and Teotihuacan motifs. It is especially dramatic when floodlit at night.

The Shrine Auditorium (at 665 West Jefferson Boulevard) was built in 1927, and at that time it was the biggest theater

The Mayan Theater today. The brightly painted 1927 building was originally a light gray. The paint job accentuates the allure of Francisco Comeja's seven "warrior-priests" looming above the entrance. Originally a musical-comedy venue, it later became a salsa club. (Courtesy of the Library of Congress, Prints and Photographs Division, photograph by Carol M. Highsmith [LC-HS503-503].)

in the world, holding more than six thousand spectators. Its appearance was extremely exotic, like a huge mosque with a double dome on the outside, and a vast Moorish palace inside. This is where King Kong was put on display (in the 1933 RKO film), with the building pretending to be a Broadway theater.

Finally, at 615 South Broadway there is "the most beautiful theater in the world," the Los Angeles Theatre, built in 1931. It has a massive columned facade and a dazzlingly splendid interior with chandeliers, huge mirrors, fluted columns, and a crystal fountain. The theater opened with Charlie Chaplin's *City Lights*

(1931), one of the last major silent movies ever made, and one of the most glamorous premieres.

So what would an alien archaeologist, wholly ignorant of the "Hollywood Culture," be able to deduce from what we have just described? Obviously almost nothing. Most of the early studios are gone, replaced by offices, banks, supermarkets, and parking lots. The Lasky-DeMille Barn is a small building filled with strange artifacts and old photographs. The front of the Chaplin studio looks like a row of Tudor cottages. An occasional plaque, such as those for Walt Disney's or Hal Roach's studio, informs one that something happened on these spots, but a phrase such as "Laugh Factory to the World" does not really afford any clues as to exactly what was produced here, even if one could read and understand the language. Even the huge modern studios, with their soundstages, might not be readily recognizable to an alien visitor. Certainly, iconic monuments such as the Paramount gate would be meaningless—merely examples of idiosyncratic and elegant design.

Likewise the great sets are all gone, and the reconstructed bit of the Babylon set on Hollywood Boulevard would not be understood—what relevance has Babylon, let alone elephant statues, to the middle of Hollywood? As for the staircase and the Laurel and Hardy houses, they would not be of the slightest interest except as examples of architecture and design to an alien archaeologist without precise knowledge of the relevant Laurel and Hardy films.

And what of the great theaters? They might well be recognized as places of mass entertainment or, more probably, of mass worship, which is not too far from the truth. But why such a vast variety in their designs, from Egyptian to Chinese to Mayan to Moorish to Art Deco? And why such incredible opulence? Did the faithful contribute money toward the decoration of the theaters as a sign of respect to the gods? Or were they a display of wealth by a number of different rulers who provided enter-tainment to the people, rather like rich Romans financing lavish games?

In the next chapter, we shall see if further clues are available from other public buildings—the "entertainment areas."

FIVE

The Entertainment Areas

Bread and Circuses

Among the most important aspects of any archaeological culture are the evidence of diet, trade, and social life.

This chapter will therefore present a brief overview of some of the restaurants, bars, clubs, and sports facilities from Hollywood's early days—some of which survive, and many of which do not—as well as the main watering holes and food troughs of "El Lay," and its "gladiatorial arena," as well as some churches.

We shall also look at the "in places" where stars went to be seen enjoying themselves, and the appalling stores where they spent more than they could afford on things they didn't need to impress people they didn't like. This was a culture where appearance was everything—were it one's social surroundings, one's clothes, one's car, or, of course, one's house (see chapter 6).

It was also a culture which reveled in a different kind of excess. By the 1920s, cocaine had become a universal pick-me-up in Hollywood. Only a few years earlier, it had been a subject for humor when Douglas Fairbanks in 1916 played a character called Coke Ennyday in the movie *The Mystery of the Leaping Fish*. Visiting town around that time, Alistair Crowley referred to movie people as a bunch of "cocaine-crazed sexual lunatics." Inevitably drugs took their toll—for example, leading lady Barbara LaMarr, dubbed the "Girl Who Was Too Beautiful," and who had six husbands and innumerable lovers, died from an overdose of heroin at twenty-six years of age. Bela Lugosi, the star of *Dracula*, had a terrible morphine addiction which caused a long, lingering decline. Even more tragic was the case of Wallace Reid, one of the greatest stars of the early 1920s, who, while filming *The Valley of the Giants* (1919), was given morphine to relieve pain caused by injuries sustained in a train crash. Eventually he became addicted and declined to an early death in 1923.

Drink was another vice, and numerous stars more or less drank themselves to death—most famously John Barrymore, John Gilbert, W. C. Fields, and William Holden. Others, like Buster Keaton, were more fortunate in that they had an alcoholic period but managed to come through it. Which establishments catered to such excesses?

STARS AND BARS: THE WATERING HOLES AND FOOD TROUGHS

The first celebrity restaurant was John's Cafe, located in Wilcox's Hall at Hollywood and Cahuenga boulevards. For a while, it was *the* place to meet—especially as movie folk tended to eat late, and no other establishment catered to that. The early studios did not have commissaries. At the same time, businesses of other kinds were springing up along Hollywood Boulevard—hardware stores, drugstores (where movie folk could buy their makeup), and beauty parlors. By 1915 there were a hundred business premises here.

The Musso and Frank Grill, at 6667 Hollywood Boulevard, is considered the town's oldest continuously operating restaurant, having opened in 1919. It was originally called "Frank's French Cafe" or "François," and it received its current name in 1923. At first it was frequented by the likes of Gloria Swanson, Douglas Fairbanks, Mary Pickford, John Barrymore, and Cecil B. DeMille—partly because there were not too many places where one could eat in those days. For many years it was considered the finest eatery on the boulevard, albeit unglamorous. Its menu was extensive, and its food well-prepared. In the 1930s it was a favorite place for writers and playwrights such as F. Scott Fitzgerald, Lillian Hellman, Dashiell Hammett, Aldous Huxley, Dorothy Parker, Dalton Trumbo, and Ernest Hemingway.

The Musso and Frank Grill today.

Henry's, a restaurant at 6315 Hollywood Boulevard, was financed by Charlie Chaplin and run by Henry Bergman, an actor from Chaplin's comedies. It was particularly popular as the first Hollywood restaurant to be open after midnight, and it was often frequented by Al Jolson after the Friday night boxing matches at Legion Stadium.

The famous Brown Derby restaurant (at 3377 Wilshire Boulevard) was built in 1926 as a coffee shop by Gloria Swanson's second husband, Herbert K. Somborn. Three more were later constructed: at 9537 Wilshire Boulevard in Beverly Hills; at 4500 Los Feliz Boulevard (1941); and at 1628 North Vine Street (1929)—it was in this one that Clark Gable proposed to Carole Lombard—but all are now long gone. The shopping mall on the site of the original Brown Derby has a brown dome as a poor reminder of past glories. Nobody really knows the origin of the restaurants' name. One story is that New York Governor Al Smith was wearing a brown derby on a visit to his friend Somborn in Los Angeles. Another is that someone challenged Somborn, saying, "If you know anything about food, you can sell it out of a hat." Or perhaps it was just that the derby hat was a symbol of upper-middle-class social respectability!

Cocoanut Grove (many spell it "Coconut")—opened in 1921 and decorated with a forest of fake palm trees supposedly salvaged from the set of Rudolph Valentino's *The Sheik*—was located in the Ambassador Hotel, and it was one of Hollywood's most glamorous and famous nightspots. Bing Crosby's singing career began here. The Academy Awards ceremony was held there on six occasions in the 1930s and 1940s. As we shall see in the next chapter, this famous and historic location has been almost obliterated.

As early Hollywood had no nightlife at all, in 1922 Rudolph Valentino himself paid for The Little Club, at 7016 Hollywood

The original Brown Derby restaurant, which opened in 1926, on Wilshire Boulevard in Los Angeles. This photograph is dated October 29, 1957. There were several Brown Derby restaurants in the city, but this was the only one with a derby shape. (Bettmann/CORBIS)

Boulevard, where there was dancing till midnight to the strains of a nine-piece orchestra. Unfortunately, the Boulevard still had numerous homes at that time, and so many residents complained at having their sleep disturbed and being kept awake that the place quickly closed!

Hollywood's first true nightclub was the Montmartre Café (at 6757 Hollywood Boulevard)—it opened in 1923 and was a great success for years. One could see Rudolph Valentino dancing there, or Charlie Chaplin chatting to Marion Davies. Joan Crawford was discovered here. It gradually became a tourist trap, with fans, eager to see their favorite stars, crowding around the front door, jostling the celebrities, or gawping at them as they ate. In 1930, a new and exclusive club, the Embassy, was built next door for a very limited clientele of only three hundred (including Charlie Chaplin, Gloria Swanson, John Gilbert, and Norma Talmadge). Once the stars had moved to the Embassy, the Montmartre lost its appeal to tourists, and its owner filed for bankruptcy. The new owner managed to revive it by featuring musicians such as Hoagy Carmichael and the Rhythm Boys—one of the latter was Bing Crosby, who met his first wife, Dixie Lee, there. Eventually the public were allowed into the Embassy Club, which killed it along with the Montmartre.

The Trocadero Cafe Restaurant was opened in 1934 at 8610 Sunset Boulevard, and it was one of the most popular nightclubs of Hollywood until it closed in 1946. Judy Garland, Deanna

The Montmartre Café's building today.

Durbin, and many others entertained there. This is where David Selznick celebrated the opening of *Gone with the Wind* in 1939. It was torn down years ago, with only its three front-door steps surviving for a while at the southeast corner of Sunset Boulevard and Sunset Plaza.

The Mocambo nightclub opened in 1939 at 8588 Sunset Boulevard and was a favorite with the movie industry until it closed in 1958. Édith Piaf and Lena Horne sang here. It is now, inevitably, a parking lot. Ciro's, which was Hollywood's biggest and grandest nightclub, was also opened in 1939 at 8433 Sunset Boulevard; it has now become the Comedy Store.

Chasen's Restaurant (at 9039 Beverly Boulevard) opened in 1937 and was a favorite of many stars such as W. C. Fields, Errol Flynn, and Humphrey Bogart. Another roadside diner was the location of one of Hollywood's most mysterious deaths. Thelma Todd, a glamorous actress known as the "Ice Cream Blonde," appeared in many comedies in the 1920s and 1930s, including some with Laurel and Hardy. She opened a restaurant, Thelma Todd's Beach Sidewalk Cafe, at 17575 Pacific Coast Highway, and lived in an apartment above it. In December 1935, after an evening at a glamorous Hollywood party at the Trocadero Cafe Restaurant, she was found dead—still in her gown, fur coat, and diamonds—in her Lincoln Phaeton car in its small garage. Debate still rages as to whether she killed herself or was murdered. One theory is that the Mafia killed her for refusing to let them use her café as a gambling den. The café, a fine Spanish building with a tiled roof, still stands unchanged on the highway—in recent years it has been a center for making religious films.

Many of Hollywood's most noteworthy eating places have disappeared over the years, and one of the saddest losses was the Hollywood Canteen (at 1451 North Cahuenga Boulevard, just south of Sunset), a truly historic place founded by Bette

Thelma Todd's Beach Sidewalk Cafe as it looks today.

Davis and John Garfield in 1942. This was where hundreds of thousands of servicemen were entertained in a nightclub run by movie stars during World War II. The building had been a stable, and then a little theater, and it was rented for $100 a month. Hundreds of volunteers reworked and equipped it for its new function. There were tables, chairs, a stage, a dance floor, and a snack bar. The walls were decorated with murals and cartoons by famous artists. It opened on October 3, 1942, with Eddie Cantor acting as master of ceremonies. Any uniform from the armed forces was given admission, and all refreshments inside were free. Over one six-month period, more than 600 stars entertained there, while 100,000 young men visited the Canteen every month. GIs might find their table waited on by Hedy Lamarr, Betty Grable, Dorothy Lamour, or Marlene Dietrich. Frank Sinatra sang there, Danny Kaye often entertained, and Orson Welles did magic tricks including sawing Rita Hayworth, his new wife, in half! Davis herself did everything from

The now vanished Hollywood Canteen, circa 1943. (Courtesy of hollywood photographs.com.)

waiting tables to scrubbing floors. Over its three-year lifespan, the Canteen was open every day and entertained about three million servicemen and -women, but it closed on August 14, 1945, when news of the Japanese surrender arrived. Unfortunately the historic Canteen is now a five-story parking garage.

STORES FOR STARS: RODEO DRIVE AND OTHER SYMBOLS OF WEALTH

Rodeo Drive has become one of the most expensive shopping streets in the world, with stores from end to end, and no prices in the windows. If you need to ask the price, why are you shopping here? This hugely expensive retail street and real estate area began as a bridle path, and Greta Garbo used to jog here in the 1930s! This is the heart of Beverly Hills, which has been called the most fabulous six square miles on the planet, thanks to the movie-star houses (see chapter 6), the wealth and fame, and the expensive cars. Beverly Hills was supposedly named after Beverly Farms in Massachusetts. In 1910 it only had a few houses. The erection of the Beverly Hills Hotel in 1912 brought more visitors, but by 1920 the population was still only seven hundred. It was only the arrival of the "King and Queen of Hollywood," at Pickfair, which really put it on the map, leading many other stars to follow.

As the movie industry grew, and fortunes started to be made by producers, directors, and the big stars, ostentatious status-symbol automobiles were in great demand. Actor S. I. Hayakawa owned a gold-plated Pierce-Arrow limousine. Francis X. Bushman had a lavender Rolls-Royce with gold door-handles and his gold monogram on the door. He was driven around by a chauffeur in a lavender uniform, while smoking lavender cigarettes. Two of the most remarkable celebrity cars remain in the Hollywood area, forming part of the remarkable Nethercutt Collection, on show for free in the Nethercutt Museum in Sylmar.

One of them is the red 1923 McFarlan Knickerbocker Cabriolet owned by Roscoe "Fatty" Arbuckle, which cost $9,000 in 1923 (another of Arbuckle's cars, a blue 1919 Pierce-Arrow, still survives in the United States and was recently put up for auction; bidding reached $1.1 million, but it was not sold). The other is Rudolph Valentino's 1923 Voisin Sporting Victoria, which would have cost him $14,000 at that time. Valentino loved fast, exotic, sporty cars, and after his arrival in Hollywood in 1916—when he was a total unknown and was struggling to survive as a movie extra—he used to hang out with Italian mechanics at the automobile businesses that were springing up along Hollywood Boulevard. They sometimes let him borrow flashy cars to impress his friends!

In 1923, at the height of his career, Valentino visited Paris on his honeymoon with his second wife, Natacha Rambova, and test-drove every automobile available. He finally chose the Voisin and bought not one but three. He left two in Paris and brought one to Hollywood, where it can still be seen, in immaculate condition. Its hood ornament is a coiled cobra, a gift to him from Douglas Fairbanks, in honor of Valentino's latest film at the time, *Cobra*. One of the few "artifacts" of the Golden Age to survive in Hollywood, this magnificent car is displayed alongside a photograph of Valentino posing proudly alongside it in 1924 with one of his beloved dogs.

GLADIATORS AND SAINTS: GRAPPLES AND CHAPELS

The "Tower of Babylon," the former Hollywood Athletic Club (at 6525 Sunset Boulevard and Hudson Avenue), was a favorite with male stars from the 1920s to the 1950s. Its Olympic-size, twenty-five-yard swimming pool was used by Clark Gable, John Gilbert, and Robert Taylor. Rudolph Valentino stayed here whenever he had a disagreement with one of his wives. John Barrymore and John Wayne had drinking parties in the penthouse rooms. It is now an office building.

The Hollywood Legion Stadium (at 1628 El Centro Avenue) was the place where the stars went on Friday evenings to see boxing matches—Valentino, Chaplin, Harlow, Chaney,

Gable, and Bogart were regulars—but it was turned into a bowling alley in 1960.

The Hollywood Studio Club (at 6129 Carlos Avenue), established in 1916 and located in an old house, was the home for many aspiring young actresses who came from all over the country to seek stardom—actresses such as ZaSu Pitts, Mae Busch, and Janet Gaynor. It was founded by Cecil B. DeMille's wife and Mary Pickford. It was moved in 1926 to 1215 Lodi Place, where its occupants included Kim Novak and Sharon Tate; Marilyn Monroe had room 334 in 1948. The original building has been replaced by a parking lot.

On a site often used by makers of silent movies for filming cheap Westerns, an outdoor amphitheater named the Hollywood Bowl (at 2301 North Highland Avenue) was created by Christine

The Hollywood Bowl.

Wetherill Stevenson, heiress to the Pittsburgh Paint Company. She wanted the amphitheater to be used for religion rather than light music, and so she planned a series of religious dramas, but her main impact was the establishment of the Easter Passion Play. The Hollywood Bowl held its first concert in 1921. A new shell designed by Frank Lloyd Wright was commissioned for it in 1927, and it used lumber and plasterboard from the sets of *Robin Hood*, donated by Pickford-Fairbanks Studios. Today this famous outdoor amphitheater remains a major entertainment center for Hollywood residents and thousands of tourists.

Hollywood, did, of course, contain many more traditional places for religious observance. In the Wilcox era, churches began to spring up among the houses and farms. The first to get themselves organized were German Methodists who, ironically, built a church on a former lemon grove at the southeast corner of Hollywood Boulevard and Vine Street, an intersection which would much later become a byword for vice and decadence! By the time the movie industry turned up, every Christian denomination had a church along Hollywood Boulevard. None of them was to survive there.

One church has been the scene of so many major events linked to the movie industry's stars that it deserves special mention. The Church of the Good Shepherd at 505 North Bedford Drive in Beverly Hills has been the main place of worship for Catholic movie stars since it was dedicated in 1925. Among the marriages it has seen were those of Carmen Miranda in 1947, and in 1950 that of an eighteen-year-old Elizabeth Taylor and Nicky Hilton (the marriage lasted three months). There have also been some spectacular funerals here, from that of Rudolph Valentino in 1926 to those of Gary Cooper (1961), Rosalind Russell (1976), Peter Finch (1977), Jimmy Durante (1980), Alfred Hitchcock (1980), and Frank Sinatra (1998).

The Church of the Good Shepherd.

Could any of the above-mentioned sites give our alien archaeologist any kind of clue to the role and importance of the "Hollywood Culture"? Not really. Most of them have been obliterated, as usual. Those which are left provide no real information—restaurants and churches and shops may be recognized for their basic functions, but they provide no information about the very special people who frequented them. Only the opulent cars, which are clearly symbols of wealth, indicate that some individuals in this culture acquired enormous resources which could be spent on such expensive toys. These clues will receive further confirmation from the evidence examined in chapter 6, the residential areas.

SIX

The Residential Area
The Original Beverly Hillbillies

We now turn to the surviving clues of domestic life, the idiosyncratic architecture in this "Queen City of Plastic," an aspect of the culture in which megalomania and snobbery were rampant. The standard technique, as in many ancient cultures, was a "teardown" in which previous buildings were demolished, regardless of their history or architectural merits, to be replaced by something far grander, at least in the new owners' eyes. It is ironic that Hollywood is sometimes referred to as "Babylon" since some of the original Babylon was similarly torn down and replaced by a monument to the glory of Saddam Hussein.

GILDED GHETTOS: THE HOUSES

Beverly Hills was originally named by Burton Green, president of the Rodeo Land and Water Company, which planned it as a strictly upper-class place. The first home was built there in

1904, but three years later there were still only six. But the building of the Beverly Hills Hotel in 1912 began to attract more inhabitants to the town. Today, as one goes north from Sunset Strip, the nightclubs, restaurants, and office buildings rapidly give way to tree-shaded streets, huge lawns, and mansions, some of them pseudo-reproductions of Greek and Roman villas with columns and statues.

The most famous dwelling in Hollywood was Pickfair, the home of Mary Pickford and Douglas Fairbanks, the first King and Queen of Hollywood. Located at 1143 Summit Drive, Pickfair was originally built in 1911 by an attorney, Lee Phillips, as a six-room hunting lodge with no running water or electricity. Fairbanks bought it in 1919 for $38,000, and asked his art director, Max Parker, to transform it into a huge forty-two-room mansion, which he presented to his new bride, known as "America's Sweetheart," in 1920. Its one-hundred-foot swimming pool was the first built in Beverly Hills. By the mid-1920s Fairbanks and Pickford were receiving other royalty at their house—including

Pickfair then (postcard).

the last king of Spain, Alfonso XIII; King Umberto of Italy; and the king and queen of Siam—while their parties were frequented by the likes of Rudolph Valentino, Anna Pavlova, Albert Einstein, Greta Garbo, George Bernard Shaw, the Mountbattens, and President Calvin Coolidge. According to *Life* magazine,

Pickfair now.

Pickfair was "only slightly less important than the White House . . . and much more fun." Among the treasures it contained were Rodin drawings, jade carvings, and a 100-piece china set inscribed, "Napoléon à Joséphine," given by Bonaparte to his bride on their wedding day. Fairbanks and Pickford divorced in 1935, and Pickford married her third husband, Buddy Rogers, at the house in 1937. After her death in 1979, aged 86, Rogers sold the property for $10 million. He had hoped to donate Pickfair to an institution such as a charity, hospital, or university but none could afford the annual upkeep of $300,000–$400,000.

A rear view of Rudolph Valentino's Hollywood home, circa 1927. It was known as Falcon Lair. The house was built on the side of a high hill, and the living and dining rooms are below the level of the street. In the left foreground is a birdhouse and on the right is a runway for the star's dogs. (Bettmann/CORBIS)

Sadly, the house was eventually sold again in 1987 for $7 million to Meshulam Riklis, whose wife, Pia Zadora, largely demolished it (claiming termite problems!) and built a new three-story $11 million mansion on the site. Even though this was a modernized version of the original, it remains one of the most horrific acts of deliberate vandalism in Hollywood's history.

Almost equally horrific was the fate of Bing Crosby's historic estate at 594 Mapleton Drive, which in 1983 was bought for $10 million by TV producer Aaron Spelling, who tore it down and constructed a six-acre $40 million 123-room mansion.

Next door to Pickfair, at 1085 Summit Drive, was Charlie Chaplin's house, a two-story Spanish-style mansion built in 1922. It is said that most things inside it used to fall apart because Chaplin employed studio carpenters when they were not busy making sets, and their expertise was in rapidly made, temporary items! Outside the house are pines and cypresses planted by Pola Negri.

The Mediterranean-style mansion used as Norma Desmond's abode in Billy Wilder's 1950 film *Sunset Boulevard* (at 641 Irving Boulevard, on the northwest corner of Wilshire Boulevard) was built in 1922, and it subsequently belonged to Mrs. J. Paul Getty. The swimming pool, so important to the movie's opening and conclusion, was built specially for the shoot, and it had to be removed afterward. The mansion was torn down in 1957 and replaced by an office building. In the movie, the house's address was 10086 Sunset Boulevard, a long way from its actual location.

Rudolph Valentino bought a thirteen-room Spanish-style mansion on a hill in Bel Air (1436 Bella Drive) for $150,000 and named it Falcon Lair after the role he was to play in *The Hooded Falcon*. Its gateposts still bear the evocative name. In 1925 when he moved in (only a year before his death from peritonitis), Valentino found that the high wall was not deterring his army of female fans, so he added floodlights, guards, and dogs, including three Great Danes and two mastiffs. He filled the house with Middle Eastern furniture, Renaissance art objects, Oriental carpets, and medieval tapestries, armor, and weapons. The estate was later rented by Gloria Swanson in the 1950s, and then owned by billionaire heiress Doris Duke, who died there in 1993.

An Italian-style villa was built in 1926 by Buster Keaton, at 1018 Pamela Drive (Beverly Hills), as a gift to his wife, actress Natalie Talmadge. It had twenty rooms, including a hidden bar (very useful during prohibition). The house subsequently belonged to Barbara Hutton, James Mason, and others. Developers have recently restored it.

"Greenacres" was built in 1928 by Harold Lloyd, the silent-film comedian, at a cost of $2 million, and it is generally reckoned to have been the most expensive, largest, and grandest home of any Hollywood star in the 1920s, or ever. The 36,000-square-foot main mansion, with forty-four rooms and twenty-six bathrooms, was built in Italian Renaissance style, and Lloyd lived there until he passed away in 1971. Around it were fifteen acres including stables, a nine-hole golf course, and an 800-foot canoe pond full of trout and bass, which was fed by a 125-foot high waterfall. The estate's formal gardens were laid out like those of a Roman emperor (and were featured as such in the 1973 movie *Westworld*). The mansion's front courtyard had an Italian fountain, and Lloyd developed a superstition about it, always insisting that his chauffeur should reverse out of the courtyard instead of circling the fountain. The only time he went around the fountain was on the night he died. Sadly, this great estate fell into decay in Lloyd's final years, and after his death it was sold to a developer who split it into fifteen lots and took out

The Harold Lloyd estate. (Courtesy of the Library of Congress, Prints and Photographs Division [HABS CAL, 19-BevH,2–2].)

the golf course. The mansion has since been owned by a series of extremely wealthy men. It can still be seen from Benedict Drive, with fountains and terraces below it, while the estate's entrance gates are as imposing as ever.

One of the most bizarre but charming dwellings in Beverly Hills, at 516 North Walden Drive, is known as the Witch's House. It was originally the administration building of Irvin Willat Studios on Washington Boulevard in Culver City, and the art director, for some reason, designed it in the 1920s to look like a Hansel-and-Gretel cottage with peaked roofs and tilting leaded windows. Often used as a set in movies, it was moved in 1931 to this site.

Some major stars lived far from Beverly Hills; for example, one of the first movie stars to buy a house in Hollywood was

The Witch's House.

Francis X. Bushman, whose large house in an orange grove had the area's first swimming pool and was located where the Chinese Theatre now stands. At 649 West Adams Boulevard is a large Tudor mansion built in 1907, which belonged to Theda

Bara (1915–1919), Norma Talmadge, and director Joseph Schenk (1924), but also to Roscoe Arbuckle (1921) at the time of his "rape scandal." Arbuckle paid $250,000 for it. The house is now a home for Catholic priests.

Harry Houdini, the magician, is said to have had an estate (2398 Laurel Canyon Boulevard) on a steep hillside. Alas, only a crumbling grand stairway and the servants' quarters survive, but some nearby residents believe that Houdini haunts the estate.

The biggest and most lavish mansion in Hollywood was built in 1928 by William Randolph Hearst for his girlfriend Marion Davies at 415 Palisades Beach Road. The three-story building, named "Ocean House," had 118 rooms, 55 bathrooms, 37 fireplaces (many from the eighteenth century), and a 110-foot swimming pool lined with Italian marble and spanned by a Venetian-style bridge. Construction began in 1926, ended in 1930, and cost $3 million, while the furnishings cost another $4 million. Some rooms dated to the sixteenth century and were shipped over from Europe—there was a British tavern dating to 1560 and an enormous ballroom from an eighteenth-century Italian palace. Davies sold the property in 1947 for $600,000, and the main house was demolished in 1956. All that remains today of this "Versailles of Hollywood" is a guesthouse (itself quite a substantial structure) and the servants' quarters. Some of Ocean House's original eighteen Ionic columns survive in front of 9370 Santa Monica Boulevard in Beverly Hills.

Nearby, at 625 Palisades Beach Road, is the mansion owned by Louis B. Mayer from 1925 to 1957. Subsequently owned by actor Peter Lawford, it was where his brother-in-law John F. Kennedy had secret meetings with Marilyn Monroe. Not far away, at 705 Palisades Beach Road, was the beach home of Douglas Fairbanks, the silent-era king of Hollywood. He died here in 1939 of a heart attack, and his body lay in state here in an ornately carved bed in front of a window overlooking the ocean.

Other houses are notorious for the violent deaths which occurred in them; for example, Ramón Novarro (1899–1968) was a silent-screen star who as a "Latin-lover" type was a rival and friend of Rudolph Valentino. He was best known for his role in the silent *Ben-Hur* (1926). Sadly, he was beaten to death in his secluded Spanish-style house at 3110 Laurel Canyon in 1968 by two young hustlers he had picked up on Hollywood Boulevard.

Benjamin "Bugsy" Siegel (1906–1947), the mobster who built the Flamingo Hotel in Las Vegas, had his head blown off by a shotgun through the windows of the living room where he was sitting in his house at 810 Linden Drive. It is thought that the Mafia suspected him of swindling them of money he had borrowed from them to build his hotel.

HOTEL CALIFORNIA: THE HOTELS

The Hollywood Hotel (at 6811 Hollywood Boulevard, on the northwest corner with Highland Avenue) was the first luxury hotel in town. Built in 1903, its first wing was a self-contained resort with thirty-three rooms, two baths, its own power station, and an ice plant. In 1905 an annex was added, which took its total capacity to 144 rooms. From 1907 its owner was Mira Hershey of the Pennsylvania chocolate family. Later it was home to many celebrities—for example, Rudolph Valentino married his first wife Jean Acker here in 1919 and occupied the honeymoon suite; after he died, endless women came to the hotel to sleep in the room he had used. The hotel rapidly became Hollywood's social center; its Dining Room of the Stars was enormously popular with silent-movie actors, and many of them had their names painted on gold stars on its ceiling. Roscoe Arbuckle thought it funny to flip pats of butter to that very ceiling! The hotel's register, filled with famous names, is now in the Smithsonian. Unfortunately the hotel was destroyed in 1956 and is now a parking lot and bank.

The Alexandria Hotel at 501 South Spring Street opened in 1906 and was considered the most elegant in Los Angeles. In the early days this hotel was the nerve center of the movie industry—casting was carried out in the bar, and deals were made in the lobby, on a Turkish carpet known as the "Million Dollar Rug." It is said that cowboy star Tom Mix once rode his horse into the lobby and over this prize carpet! And Charlie Chaplin often did improvisations in the lobby. Virtually every major Hollywood figure stayed here, from Cecil B. DeMille on his arrival in town to D. W. Griffith and an endless roll call of stars. Eventually, eclipsed by the Ambassador, the Alexandria had to close for a few years during the Depression, but it was refurbished in the 1970s. Its restored Palm Court has a huge Tiffany stained-glass ceiling.

The Beverly Hills Hotel (at 9641 Sunset Boulevard), also known as the "Pink Palace," was built in 1912 by an oilman, and at that time it stood amid bean fields and empty lots. Its current owner, the Sultan of Brunei, paid $185 million for it in 1987 and reopened it in 1995 after a $100 million renovation. Much was left intact—especially the twenty-two bungalows on the property's twelve acres of gardens. Howard Hughes used to reserve four bungalows at a time—one for himself, another for his wife, and two for decoys. Marilyn Monroe conducted her affair with Yves Montand in bungalows 21 and 22. Clark Gable had secret assignations with Carole Lombard here before they married. The hotel features a famous swimming pool, a favorite with starlets, and its legendary Polo Lounge Grill. Needless to say,

The Beverly Hills Hotel, circa 1912. (Courtesy of hollywoodphotographs.com.)

everything is extraordinarily expensive, with room rates ranging from hundreds to thousands of dollars per night.

The Ambassador Hotel (at 3400 Wilshire Boulevard) opened in 1921 on the site of a dairy farm on a dirt road bordered by bean and barley fields. Built on twenty-four acres, it was a six-story Spanish Revival building, with a grand lobby containing crystal chandeliers and an alabaster fountain. It was also the location of the famous Coco(a)nut Grove nightclub. On its grounds was a great pool with a sand "beach," and the palatial Siesta Cottage, occupied at different times by Rudolph Valentino, John Barrymore, and F. Scott and Zelda Fitzgerald. Gloria Swanson lived at the hotel, as it was owned by her second husband, Herbert K. Somborn, who built the Brown Derby opposite. Howard Hughes also lived in a bungalow here in the late 1920s. Pola Negri is said to have walked her pet cheetah on its grounds. Other guests included Charlie Chaplin, Winston

Churchill, and Albert Einstein. It was here in 1952 that Richard Nixon wrote the Checkers speech which saved his career, insisting that the only gift he had received from supporters was his cocker spaniel Checkers; and it was also here that, a decade later, after a failed attempt to become governor of California, he told a press conference, "You won't have Dick Nixon to kick around anymore." It was the scene of Robert F. Kennedy's assassination in the kitchen on June 5, 1968, and the jury for the Manson Family trial was housed here for nine months in 1969–1970. The hotel closed in 1989, and gradually its hallways became filled with graffiti. Astoundingly, this historic building was torn down in 2005 and replaced by a school! However, the Coco(a)nut

The Ambassador Hotel just after construction completion, 1924. A school currently stands on the site. (Courtesy of hollywoodphotographs.com.)

Grove's original doors and a few columns have been preserved within a theater on the school grounds.

The eleven-story Knickerbocker Hotel (at 1714 North Ivar Avenue), built in 1925, is where Harry Houdini's widow held séances on the roof in 1936 to try and contact him, as well as more normal magic conventions. It was also in the Knickerbocker that the tragic and troubled Frances Farmer had an emotional breakdown in 1943 and was carried out kicking and screaming by the police. In 1962, Irene Lentz, a famous costume designer (known simply as "Irene"), jumped to her death from the eleventh floor. D. W. Griffith, known as the "Man Who Invented Hollywood," came to live in the hotel in 1948, ignored by the industry which he had done so much to pioneer. At the age of seventy-two, he could no longer find work (he had not made a film since 1931), producers refused to meet him, and he eventually took to drink. Still a megalomaniac, he was planning a seven-hour movie called *Christ and Napoleon*, a kind of sequel to his *Intolerance*, and which would have required fifty housand extras! Unfortunately, he suffered a cerebral hemorrhage, stumbled down the stairs into the hotel's lobby, collapsed, was rushed to the hospital, and died. Only six people visited the funeral parlor to pay their respects to this great pioneer, but they included Cecil B. DeMille and John Ford. His funeral, however, which took place at the Masonic Hall at 6840 Hollywood Boulevard (at Orange Avenue), attracted six hundred of the movie world's foremost directors and stars, and work at all studios stopped for three minutes. Griffith was buried in his native Kentucky. The Knickerbocker Hotel subsequently became a retirement hotel.

The Garden of Allah (8150–8152 Sunset Boulevard at Crescent Heights), opened in 1926 by the popular actress Alla Nazimova, was a hotel-apartment complex which was launched with a lavish eighteen-hour party. It had bungalows and pools and was lived in by more stars than anywhere else in Hollywood—stars including Ramón Novarro, Errol Flynn, F. Scott Fitzgerald, the Marx Brothers, Tallulah Bankhead, and Clara Bow. The Depression caused Nazimova to lose everything she had invested in the hotel. After she died in 1945, it continued as a hotel, but acquired a questionable reputation, becoming known for robbery, murder, suicide, drunkenness, fights, and orgies. Despite some protests, it was torn down in 1959, after a final party which attracted almost a thousand people, many of them imitating the stars who were associated with this fabled place. The fixtures and fittings were sold off at a public auction, with Errol Flynn's bed being the most popular item. The site is now a Chase Bank and parking lot—a piece of destruction which is thought to have inspired Joni Mitchell's "Big Yellow

The Garden of Allah Hotel in West Hollywood, 1936. A bank currently stands on the site.

Taxi" lyric "They paved paradise / And put up a parking lot." A plastic model of the hotel used to be displayed outside, and subsequently inside, the bank—but even that model has now gone.

The Roosevelt Hotel (at 7000 Hollywood Boulevard), named after Theodore Roosevelt, was built in 1927 and is still one of the finest hotels. This is where the Academy of Motion Picture Arts and Sciences, created in 1927 by Louis B. Mayer to relieve studio workers from organizing labor unions, had its first offices; and the very first Academy Awards ceremony was held here in May 1929 in the Blossom Suite. It was also in the Roosevelt (as well as elsewhere) that Clark Gable and Carole Lombard conducted their affair before marrying. Marilyn Monroe did her first commercial photography job by the pool and was often to be seen sitting in the lobby.

The Chateau Marmont (at 8221 Sunset Boulevard), an exclusive residential hotel, opened in 1929 on what was still a dirt road, and it was a favorite with stars such as Jean Harlow, Greta Garbo, Boris Karloff, and Errol Flynn. Howard Hughes was also a regular, and Billy Wilder lived here on his arrival from Europe in 1934. In March 1982 John Belushi died in bungalow 3 from an overdose of cocaine and heroin.

The Château Elysée (at 5930 Franklin Avenue) was called Hollywood's most beautiful building, and during the 1930s and 1940s was its most exclusive hotel-apartment building. The seven-story edifice was built in 1929 and contained seventy-seven apartments. Many major stars were residents here at some time, from Clark Gable and Carole Lombard to Humphrey Bogart, Edward G. Robinson, Errol Flynn, and Ginger Rogers. In the 1950s and 1960s it was a retirement home, but now it belongs to the Scientology organization (along with quite a few other important Hollywood buildings).

The Roosevelt Hotel today.

If alien archaeologists were to study the houses of the "Hollywood Culture," it would become readily apparent that enormous wealth was possessed by some residents but also that much demolition and rebuilding had taken place on some

The Chateau Marmont today.

sites—for reasons unknown, except that some edifices became ever grander and bigger. The enormous variety of architectural styles would doubtless be extremely puzzling. How would the archaeologists interpret the vast range of house types in this small area? What would they make, for example, of Fountain Avenue, one block south of Sunset Boulevard, a 1920s collection of apartment houses like turreted French châteaux alongside Moorish palaces, Spanish haciendas, and art-deco towers? The "Hollywood Culture" clearly made unique contributions to the field of architecture, and none more unique than the Witch's House, which is so different from the rest that it might have been the dwelling of a shaman!

There were also some very strange features on the grounds; for example, Liberace's backyard pool on Valley Vista Boulevard in North Hollywood was built in the shape of a grand piano, with eighty-eight black-and-white keys painted at the shallow end. More bizarrely, when Mary Astor lived on Hayvenhurst Avenue in Encino from 1943 to 1956, she had a turtle-shaped pool built, with the diving board as its head, and four stairways as its feet.

Naturally, the houses and hotels would be recognized as such, but nothing could possibly be deduced about their famous occupants, let alone about the tragedies and murders which took place in some of them. The wanton destruction of so many historic buildings could only suggest that they were of little value to the Hollywoodians, which is sadly all too true, but it is encouraging that in our own culture increasing numbers of people are taking an active interest in preserving what is left, while numerous visitors still pay to take tours around the "stars' homes," even though very few stars still live in the area, and despite the fact that many of the most historic houses are long gone.

In short, our alien archaeologists still have very little idea as to precisely what the "Hollywood Culture" was all about. Our next category of evidence, the monuments and cult centers, may present them with some clues.

SEVEN

Hollywood Hieroglyphics
Cult Centers and Sacred Rituals

Another vital area to investigate in any ancient culture is its "cognitive archaeology," or archaeology of the mind: the clues to religion and cults—How did this culture see the world? What were this people's beliefs?

THE HOLLYWOOD SIGN

One cult center which has been unique for a long time is the giant hillside sign, Hollywood's monument to itself, one of the most iconic and recognizable landmarks in the United States and indeed the world. Located high on Mount Lee, it was originally erected in 1923 at a cost of $21,000 as a promotional tool for a real estate venture headed by Mack Sennett, the "King of Comedy," a housing development called Hollywoodland, at the foot of the hill. The last four letters were eventually removed in 1945 by the Hollywood Chamber of Commerce to make the sign

In 1923, Los Angeles publisher Harry Chandler and movie star Mack Sennett developed houses in Hollywood Hills. The tract's promotional sign, each of whose letters stands four stories high, read "Hollywoodland." It was shortened in the 1940s. (Courtesy of the Library of Congress, Prints and Photographs Division, photograph by Carol M. Highsmith [LC-HS503-543].)

represent the whole city. The original letters were about thirty feet wide and almost fifty feet high, made of sheet-metal panels painted white and attached to a framework of scaffolding and wires. At one time, almost five thousand lightbulbs illuminated the sign, flashing on and off in the dark, making it a useful navigational landmark for aircraft at night. On a clear day it could be seen for twenty-five miles.

The sign was not originally made to last. In 1939 its maintenance was discontinued, and all the lightbulbs were stolen. It was vandalized, and holes appeared in the panels. Though it was declared a historic cultural monument in 1973 by the Los Angeles Cultural Heritage Board, it was an eyesore badly in need of repair by then—it had grown dilapidated, shabby, and covered with graffiti. The chamber of commerce launched a campaign to raise the money for repairs, and many groups and individuals contributed help and funds, including Hugh Hefner, Alice Cooper, Andy Williams, and Gene Autry. Each letter cost $27,700 to reconstruct. The new sign was unveiled on November 11, 1978. Nowadays it looks splendid and pristine, but it can only be viewed from a distance—visitors are no longer welcome. It is 450 feet long, with letters 45 feet high, and weighs 480,000 pounds. It has been called "Hollywood's Eiffel Tower." And like the Eiffel Tower, the sign has often been used in different kinds of advertising; for example, in September 1987, to mark a visit by the Pope, jokers wrapped black plastic around the first L to change the name to HOLYWOOD. Earlier that same year,

Part of the Hollywood sign in 1985, showing graffiti.

in May, pranksters from the California Institute of Technology went to the sign at dead of night and draped parts of it with plastic so that it read CALTECH, proclaiming this a "100th anniversary present for Hollywood"! In 1990, advertisements for Virgin Atlantic's newly announced direct flights to Los Angeles featured a doctored photo of the sign which read JOLLYGOOD!

The sign has also known its share of tragedy, most famously the case of Peg Entwhistle, an English actress who came out to Hollywood—after both success and disaster on the Broadway stage—to seek fame and fortune. She had a few mediocre roles in RKO films, but the studio decided not to pick up her option in July 1932. She lived with her uncle in a modest house at 2428 Beachwood Drive. It is said that she used to stand at its gate in

The house from which Peg Entwhistle gazed at the Hollywood sign and from which she began her last journey.

the evening and gaze up at the sign which looms above the end of the street. On the evening of September 16, 1932, she told her uncle that she was going out to buy cigarettes—but instead she went up to the sign, climbed the H, and jumped off . . . She was twenty-four years old. Very few people attended her funeral.

Surprisingly, there are very few monuments to the film industry or filmmakers in Hollywood. The only star to have a statue is Rudolph Valentino, whose monument and bust are in De Longpre Park (Cherokee Avenue at De Longpre Avenue). After Valentino's death in 1926, a campaign was launched to raise funds for the erection of a monument to the star. Subscriptions came in from all over the world, and so the sculptor Roger Noble received the commission to produce a statue. Titled *Aspiration*, it was dedicated on May 6, 1930, the anniversary of Valentino's birth. Four feet high, this bronze of a nude male, its head stretching to the heavens, stands on a globe of green marble, and the inscription below reads, "Erected in memory of Rudolph Valentino, 1895–1926. Presented by his friends and admirers from every walk of life in all parts of the world. In appreciation of the happiness brought to them by his cinema portrayals." The statue was stolen from its pedestal in the 1950s but was later recovered and kept in storage for safety. It was finally restored to its pedestal in 1976. A bronze bust of Valentino stands nearby.

At the intersection of Olympic Boulevard and Beverly Drive is the Monument to the Motion Picture People Who Helped Save Beverly Hills. Topped by a spiraling piece of film, its base features costumed bas-relief figures of Mary Pickford, Douglas Fairbanks, Rudolph Valentino, Tom Mix, Harold Lloyd, Will Rogers, Conrad Nagel, and Frank Niblo. They were so honored in 1959 because in 1923, as residents of Beverly Hills, they

The Valentino monument.

helped persuade their neighbors to refuse a plan by Los Angeles to annex their city.

A more recent monument, comprising a giant loop of film made of stainless steel, is the "Heart of Screenland." Set within a fountain on the corner of Overland Avenue and Culver Boule-

The Valentino bust.

vard in Culver City, it was built in 1981 in front of the Veterans Memorial Building, opposite what used to be an MGM back lot. A plaque states that it is "dedicated by the citizens of Culver City—The Motion Picture Capital of the World."

The Monument to the Motion Picture People Who Helped Save Beverly Hills.

GETTING UNDER PEOPLE'S FEET:
STARS ON THE SIDEWALK

We now turn to one of the real cult centers: in the heart of Hollywood, along both sides of Hollywood Boulevard, there is a

The Monument to the Motion Picture People Who Helped Save Beverly Hills, showing the bas-reliefs of Rogers, Pickford, and Fairbanks.

sidewalk of grey terrazzo in which are large brass-and-pink terrazzo stars. What could these possibly mean? What does this symbol denote? Each star bears capital letters and also one of a small series of strange motifs. Of course, this is the famous "star

The Heart of Screenland Monument.

pavement"—but, on reflection, why do we refer to celebrities as "stars"? Does it mean that they shine brightly like remote suns, bringing a little illumination into our sad lives? Or would our alien archaeologist suppose the people of the "Hollywood Culture" believed that movie stars were gods who had descended from the heavens to enthrall us? In fact, surprisingly, the term "stars" has been applied to celebrities since the nineteenth century, and possibly even the eighteenth!

The sidewalk stars were first proposed in 1953 by the Hollywood Chamber of Commerce as a way to pay homage to the artists who helped make Hollywood the most famous and glamorous place in the world. The first eight were set in place in 1960 at the northwest corner of Hollywood Boulevard and Highland, and they included Burt Lancaster, Ronald Colman, and Joanne

Here and following pages: Various stars on the Hollywood Walk of Fame. (Frank Sinatra star and Kirk Douglas star photographs are courtesy of the Library of Congress, Prints and Photographs Division, photographs by Carol M. Highsmith [LC-DIG-highsm-1765 and LC-DIG-highsm-24280].)

Woodward. There are now more than 2,100 of them. Each bears the name of a celebrity—mostly movie actors and actresses, together with a few cartoon characters, television performers, and musicians. The strange motif below the name indicates whether they worked in motion pictures, television, radio, recording, or live theater. It is doubtless wonderful for the ego to have one's own star, but those who are so "honored" by the Hollywood Chamber of Commerce have to pay thousands of dollars for the privilege! Even so, about fifteen to twenty stars are added annually, and this is one of Hollywood's foremost tourist attractions.

From the golden age of Hollywood, one can see the stars for Rudolph Valentino (6164 Hollywood), D. W. Griffith (6535), Mary Pickford (6280), Douglas Fairbanks (7022), Mabel Normand (6821), Jean Harlow (6910), Mack Sennett (6710), Charlie Chaplin (6751), Roscoe Arbuckle (6701). Buster Keaton (6619), Harry Langdon (6927), Gloria Swanson (6750), Carole

Lombard (6930), Stan Laurel (7021), Oliver Hardy (1500 Vine), Harold Lloyd (1503 Vine), and Hal Roach (1654 Vine). Doubtless the most popular of all is the star of Marilyn Monroe (6774 Hollywood).

Our alien archaeologists might also be puzzled by the fact that among the stars—if they can decipher the writing—are those for a mouse called Mickey (6925 Hollywood), a duck called Donald (6834), and a bunny called Bugs (7007)!

MAKING AN IMPRESSION:
THE CHINESE THEATRE PRINTS

Another astonishing phenomenon which an alien archaeologist would encounter on Hollywood Boulevard is the forecourt of a Chinese-style building which is filled with scores of sets of footprints and handprints and with writing on the ground. In recent years it has been fashionable for some misguided souls to see all handprints in rock art as an attempt to reach through a rock "veil" to touch a spirit world beyond. It certainly looks as though the people of the "Hollywood Culture" were obsessed with reaching through this veil, even jumping feetfirst through it! And it would likewise be clear to the aliens that semi-centaurs existed in this culture—in three cases the two human handprints are accompanied by two human footprints and two horse hoof-prints! These would thus obviously be therianthropes—crea-tures that are part human and part animal—and therefore sha-mans, according to our alien archaeologists. There are certainly therianthropes to be seen on Hollywood Boulevard even to-day—indeed, I encountered a pair of them on my last visit: a pair of mouse-human hybrids, one of whom was wearing a sorcerer's hat, which certainly suggested that they were shamans (on closer inspection, however, they turned out to be a couple dressed as Mickey and Minnie Mouse for the benefit of tourist cameras).

The true explanation, of course, is that this is Grauman's famous Chinese Theatre, since 1927 and even today the glamorous setting for movie premieres (see chapter 4). Its forecourt has a world-famous pavement of movie-star prints and signatures. The tradition of making them supposedly began through an accident in 1927 when Norma Talmadge, a star of silent movies, came to the site to see how the building's construction was making progress, and stepped out of the automobile into a patch of wet cement. Grauman immediately had Norma and her companions Douglas Fairbanks and Mary Pickford imprint their hand- and footprints, and the cult began. This is an enduring myth, but the truth is said to be less glamorous and more prosaic—Sid Grauman himself had walked across the forecourt's freshly laid cement, and his chief mason confronted him and scolded him for it. This gave Grauman a brilliant idea, and he immediately invited Fairbanks, Pickford, and Talmadge to come and make their prints in the center of the forecourt.

It is said that the prints attracted more than half a million visitors in the first four months alone, so this was a stroke of genius on Grauman's part, and the collection grew steadily from then on. However, if a star's fame diminished—and that happened quite often—their prints were quietly removed at night and replaced by those of someone more popular.

Even today, the rare invitation to add one's prints to this amazing autograph album is seen as the ultimate accolade. For the public, the prints are a chance to prove that the magnified images on the screen are actually no bigger than anyone else and are often far smaller than we think. The young Marilyn Monroe liked to come here and stand in the footprints. Personally, I have

Prints in the forecourt of the Chinese Theatre. Pictured: the prints of Gene Autry and his horse, Champ.

found that my own hands are exactly the same size as those of Arnold Schwarzenegger!

The above-mentioned semi-centaurs are the prints of movie cowboys Tom Mix, Gene Autry, and Roy Rogers together with those of their horses Tony, Champ, and Trigger. It is puzzling that there are only two hoofprints per horse. In addition, Clarence "Ducky" Nash has duck-prints; there are robotic prints from *Star Wars*; and there are the paw-prints of Uggie, the dog from *The Artist*. Other stars left similarly offbeat prints, such as Sonja Henie's ice skates and Jimmy Durante's nose ("Sid, dis is my schnozzle"). Once again, what would an alien archaeologist deduce from all these?

Prints in the forecourt of the Chinese Theatre: Tom Mix and his horse, Tony.

Prints in the forecourt of the Chinese Theatre: Roy Rogers and his horse, Trigger.

Mary Pickford (center) and Douglas Fairbanks (right) creating their prints in 1927. (Courtesy of hollywoodphotographs.com.) Sid Grauman is at left.

More of the prints in the forecourt of the Chinese Theatre. Pictured: Norma Talmadge.

More of the prints in the forecourt of the Chinese Theatre. Pictured: Jimmy Durante.

Charlie Chaplin's prints located at his own studio.

More than two million people a year visit these prints—making it one of the most important places of pilgrimage in the world. One major star who never placed his footprints here was Charlie Chaplin, who preferred to make his marks in cement within his own studio, where they can still be seen. In recent years, a similar practice of leaving prints and signatures in cement has arisen in the lobby of the Vista Theatre (see chapter 3), where they include those of the great Ray Harryhausen.

Finally, the stores on and around Hollywood Boulevard sell many other kinds of goods depicting the "gods"—posters, postcards, T-shirts, fridge magnets, figurines, and all kinds of junk are on sale. Even books!

Our alien archaeologists must be really baffled by now. What is one to make of a giant sign on a hillside? It could be a tribal symbol, or perhaps it's the name of an egomaniacal ruler. What do the hundreds of star shapes along both sides of a road denote? What do the different symbols on them mean? And why are there so many hand- and footprints and scripts collected in two places? Are these prayers requesting help from the gods or votive offerings in thanks for services obtained? It is unlikely that the aliens would realize that these were the marks of the "gods" themselves! As for the monuments in Hollywood, why are there so few of them? And what is the significance of the loops of a long flat material, with tiny perforations running along both edges? To anyone unfamiliar with spools of film, how could one possibly imagine the concept of moving pictures using that medium?

There is one last category of evidence awaiting our archaeologist: the necropolises scattered throughout the area. What will they tell us about the enigmatic people of the "Hollywood Culture"?

EIGHT

Stardust

Cities of the Dead

Study of the dead and how they were treated has always been of fundamental importance to archaeology. Although in this case we cannot actually excavate the dead, we can nevertheless learn much from their manner of disposal and their monuments— from the very simple to the ridiculously elaborate, from the tasteful private garden to the brash, vulgar edifice. Hollywood's versions of the necropolis are of enormous cultural interest, with marble and granite mausoleums and markers, and architectural styles ranging from Romanesque to Art Deco.

The burial practices in the Hollywood area were vividly presented in Tony Richardson's *The Loved One*, his 1965 film of Evelyn Waugh's 1948 novel satirizing the funeral customs of southern California. Most stars of the "Hollywood Culture" have simple graves, giving merely names and dates. A few, such as Stan Laurel and Oliver Hardy, have additional plaques, set up by fans, which explain their celebrity. Some have amusing epitaphs; for instance Joan Hackett ("Go away, I'm asleep"), and Lee Van Cleef ("The Best of the Bad"). One or two have epitaphs which refer obliquely to their role—for example, Mel Blanc, who provided the voices for the Warner Brothers cartoon characters, has "That's all folks." Billy Wilder, in reference to the ending of his most popular film, *Some Like it Hot*, has "I'm a writer but then nobody's perfect."

The more grandiose graves are certainly those which would attract the archaeologists of the future—those of Douglas Fairbanks, Mary Pickford, Marion Davies, Cecil B. DeMille, Tyrone Power, and, grandest of all, the astonishing tomb of Al Jolson. Yet by what, other than wealth or power, could such monumental graves be explained?

Most graves give no inkling of the sometimes tragic circumstances of the deceased: those who were murdered, such as Thomas Ince, William Desmond Taylor, Bugsy Siegel, Sharon Tate, and Ramón Novarro; those who committed suicide, like

The grave of Stan Laurel (Forest Lawn, Hollywood Hills), with the giant mosaic of American history in the background.

The grave of Oliver Hardy (Valhalla).

An amusing epitaph on the grave of Joan Hackett.

Billy Wilder references Some Like It Hot *in his humorous epitaph.*

Florence Lawrence and Charles Boyer; and those who met with accidental deaths (Carole Lombard, Tom Mix) or mysterious deaths (Virginia Rappe, Marilyn Monroe, Natalie Wood).

One aspect which no future archaeologist could hope to detect is which particular Hollywood graves were most visited by the public, and what the behavior of those visitors was. Some bring flowers, for example. Others bring birthday or Valentine cards, especially for Monroe and Wood. And as we shall see below, Monroe also attracts lipstick kisses and coins. Why do they come? Is it mere curiosity? Is it (as often in my own case) a way to pay respects and thanks? Or is it a kind of fantasy fulfillment—for example, when visitors see the grave of Clark Gable, are they truly visiting a distinguished actor, or do they feel they are visiting Rhett Butler? In a handful of cases, as we shall see

below, there is a veritable cult around the celebrity—most notably Rudolph Valentino and Marilyn Monroe.

Another aspect undetectable by archaeologists would be
the fact that many celebrity graves simply cannot be visited, to
the great frustration of fans, because they are in locked gardens
or mausolea, because they are left unmarked, or (as is often the
case today) because the deceased's ashes have been returned to
family or friends or scattered at sea or elsewhere.

This chapter will be a pseudo-archaeological study of the
phenomenon of the disposal of the dead in Hollywood, showing
that the size of the tomb does not always correspond to the importance of the individual during life. Even if the archaeologists
of the future were to attempt to excavate some of the countless
graves in the cemeteries here, they could not possibly learn from
them what the profession of their occupants was. (Presumably
they would focus their attention on the bigger and more grandiose monumental tombs rather than the innumerable "ordinary"
tombs.) For example, if they should chance upon the remains
of some of Hollywood's early stuntmen, they would probably
be baffled by the number of healed injuries indicated by their
skeletons (in the silent days, the average stuntman's professional
life expectancy was about five years!). What on earth could have
caused so much damage? Were they gladiators? Further, we
saw in chapter 7 that there seem to be traces of therianthropes
in Hollywood—creatures part human and part animal—and this
would certainly be confirmed by archaeological investigation of
some cemeteries.

One of the most intriguing grave markers, in the San Fernando Mission cemetery, depicts two therianthropes, both of
them duck-like with a heart symbol—an alien archaeologist
familiar with recent theory would certainly interpret these as
transforming shamans. Even more extraordinary is a grave at

The grave of Clarence "Ducky" Nash.

The grave of Isadore "Friz" Freleng.

Hillside Cemetery, which would show our alien archaeologist a whole row of different therianthropes, including creatures with features of a rabbit, duck, pig, cat, mouse, and so forth, all in elaborate clothing and apparently performing a dance of some kind. This undoubtedly would be identified as a depiction of a trance-dance performed by transforming shamans. But as with other recent and trendy archaeological theories, this would be a silly mistake. What we have here are in fact the grave of Clarence "Ducky" Nash, the man who provided the voice of Donald Duck, and that of Isadore "Friz" Freleng, one of the artists who gave us the Warner Brothers cartoons featuring Bugs Bunny, Daffy Duck, Porky Pig, Sylvester, Speedy Gonzalez, and so on. Interpreters of imagery—whether prehistoric rock art or modern—needs to be aware that humor is a fundamental human trait, and not everything in imagery, even in cemeteries, is necessarily serious or religious or mystical!

FROM HOLLYWOOD MEMORIAL PARK TO HOLLYWOOD FOREVER

Western burial practices and cemeteries reached southern California with the arrival of the Spaniards in the eighteenth century. For the first fifty years or so, burials took place in cemeteries adjoining the missions, or even inside the mission churches. There were two missions in the Los Angeles area: San Gabriel and San Fernando. As the decades passed, these cemeteries became overcrowded and dilapidated as well as malodorous, and so gradually a whole series of burial grounds were created away from residential areas, some of them designated for particular faiths—Catholic, Jewish, and so forth. In the late nineteenth century, new cemeteries had to be created farther away, as residential areas expanded.

Hollywood Memorial Park was founded in 1899 at 6000 Santa Monica Boulevard, and it is the greatest and most important cemetery of early Hollywood. Indeed, both Harvey Wilcox and his wife Daeida, who chose the name "Hollywood," are here. Today the cemetery is called Hollywood Forever. It contains some of the most grandiose tombs in the city. For example, on the island in the middle of its lake is the huge mausoleum of William A. Clark Jr. (1877–1934), founder of the Los Angeles Philharmonic Symphony Orchestra, who was a copper magnate and railroad owner. Built in 1920 in Greek style, with Ionic columns, the mausoleum cost over $250,000, the equivalent of millions today.

But easily the most important grave in this cemetery is the relatively modest resting place of one of the first "kings" or even "gods" of Hollywood, Rudolph Valentino (1895–1926). It is said that when he died, several women committed suicide. On the day of his funeral, over 100,000 people lined the streets of Los Angeles to pay homage to his cortege, and a crowd of 10,000 filled the cemetery. He was interred in a silver-bronze coffin, wearing a slave bracelet given to him by his last wife, Natacha Rambova. There were plans to build Valentino a magnificent mausoleum befitting the great star and the great screen lover, so in the meantime he was placed temporarily in this Cathedral Mausoleum vault (no. 1205) belonging to his best friend, the writer June Mathis (1892–1927). A true pioneer, Mathis was the first woman executive in the movie industry, having joined MGM in 1918 and becoming chief of the script department by 1919. She first spotted Valentino on the old Metro lot—though some accounts claim that he taught her the tango at the Hollywood Hotel—and she insisted that he be given the lead role in *The Four Horsemen of the Apocalypse*. But for some reason, Valentino's great mausoleum was never built—though he is the only

The grave of Rudolph Valentino.

star to have a monument and bust in Hollywood (see chapter 7)—and he remains in that vault to this day. Mathis joined him the following year, in the vault to the immediate left, while her husband had to go elsewhere! It is said that Valentino himself had often stood in this corner of the building, when he would bring flowers for the grave of Mathis's mother, just beneath what became his own.

For decades Valentino's grave has been associated with visits by a mysterious "Lady in Black." Every year on August 23, the anniversary of his death from peritonitis in 1926, a ghostly and heavily veiled lady would turn up to place roses at the grave. Her name was Ditra Flame (pronounced Fla-May), and it is said that as a small child she was hospitalized for a serious illness, and Valentino (who was a friend of her mother) came to visit her. Flame claimed that Valentino told her that she would outlive him, and so she should come and visit him and talk to him after his death, as he did not wish to be alone. So she kept her promise and began to go to the grave, starting in 1927, the year after his death, when she was fifteen. Eventually there were so many other women turning up on the anniversary that Flame felt superfluous and gave up in disgust in 1954; but following Elvis Presley's death in 1977, she recommenced her visits until she died in 1984 at the age of 72. Her tombstone in San Jacinto Valley Cemetery (Riverside County) identifies her as the Lady in Black.

There have been, however, other ladies in black. One, by the name of Marion Benda or Marion Watson, was a former Ziegfeld girl, and she claimed that she had a child by Valentino. Another, called Estrellita del Regil, began coming to the grave in the 1970s, and I encountered her there in February 1985, which was a somewhat spooky experience in the great, empty, echoing marble corridors of Hollywood Memorial Park's Cathedral Mausoleum. A tiny woman (4 feet 10 inches) dressed in black, with a veil, she brought roses and placed them with a theatrical flourish in the vases at either side of Valentino's plaque. Plucking up my courage, I asked her, "Did you know Rudolph Valentino?" and was then unable to escape for half an hour as she loved to talk about this, her favorite subject. I was told a torrent of stories, in her thick accent. Her answer to my question was "My muzzer was his meestress," and she gave me copies of newspaper articles about herself which she carried with her to give to people like me. She declared herself a singer, dancer, and composer who had appeared in one hundred films. She also said she was once mugged in the mausoleum!

In some of the newspaper articles she told a different story, declaring that her mother and Valentino were never intimate. She claimed that her mother, Anna Maria de Carrascosa (1910–1973), was the original Lady in Black and had been thirteen when she met Valentino. She was sitting in a New York restaurant. Valentino was at a nearby table, dressed as a gaucho, and he was immediately smitten by her beauty. He took her hand and kissed it. Anna was so young and shy that she began to cry. Valentino thought she was eighteen and wanted to marry her, but her parents refused to allow it. Perhaps this was because he was, after all, a simple Italian immigrant dishwasher before he became the biggest heartthrob the world had ever known, a man who made countless women swoon.

Anna used to make the annual pilgrimage to the grave, bringing a rosary and placing flowers. Estrellita took over the role of the Lady in Black after her mother died, having promised her that she would look after Valentino's soul. Estrellita assured me that a ghostly apparition of Valentino sometimes came to her at home, and that she spoke with him quite often. She visited his grave not annually but weekly, every Monday, placing flowers not only for Valentino but also for his older brother Alberto who died in 1981 and was buried in a different mausoleum in the same cemetery (Abbey of the Psalms). She obviously took the role extremely seriously: she told one journalist, "My heart tell me to come here every day to be with him. I sing to him, four or five songs, because I don't want him to feel lonely." Shortly after I met Estrellita, the actual anniversary of the death came around, and both she and another Lady in Black turned up, so that a bitter fight broke out, with the women throwing their roses at each other. Only in Hollywood!

Even today many people turn up on the anniversary of Valentino's death. Estrellita was forced to give up her role in 1993 due to illness—she died in 2001 and is buried, like her mother, in Hollywood Forever. Anna Maria's tomb (like that of Ditra Flame) describes her as "The Lady in Black." She was replaced in 1995 by a younger Lady in Black, Vicki Callahan, who is merely a fan. Nobody at the anniversary events these days ever knew Valentino, and few have even seen any of his twenty-two films, but such is the power of Hollywood legend that this particular cult of "the ultimate Latin lover" continues unabated.

Marion Davies (1897–1961), girlfriend of newspaper magnate William Randolph Hearst, is in the big white mausoleum by the lake, with her family name of Douras on it. To one side of it by the lake-edge is the marble monument of Tyrone Power (1914–1958), in the form of a bench with a giant book next to it with the epitaph "Good night, sweet prince, and flights of angels sing thee to thy rest." At Power's funeral, three thousand shoving fans mobbed celebrity mourners, and one woman kissed the hearse as it took the body to the grave. On the other

The tomb of Tyrone Power.

side of the Davies mausoleum, a plaque in the lawn marks the last resting place of Hannah Chaplin (1866–1928), the comedian's mother.

Also at the lake-edge is the plaque of Virginia Rappe (1896–1921), a young starlet who died after a wild party on the twelfth floor of the St. Francis Hotel in San Francisco, and whose death was falsely blamed on comedian Roscoe Arbuckle. The case was one of Hollywood's biggest scandals and it destroyed Arbuckle's career despite his innocence. Beside Rappe is producer/director Henry Lehrman (1886–1946) who was her fiancé. He visited her grave every week until his death. Janet Gaynor (1906–1984) is nearby, winner in 1929 of the first Academy Award for best actress of 1927 for *Seventh Heaven*, *Street Angel*, and *Sunrise*.

Nearby is the elegant twin crypt of Cecil B. DeMille (1881–1959) and his wife. Just behind them is a plaque for his two-year-old grandson, son of his daughter Katherine and her then-husband Anthony Quinn, who tragically drowned in a small lily pond in front of W. C. Fields's house (2015 DeMille Drive), located across the street from DeMille's own home (2000 DeMille Drive).

Not far away is the plaque of the world's "first movie star," Florence Lawrence (1886–1938), the "Biograph Girl" (after the studio for which she made many films). Previously, actors and actresses in films had been largely anonymous, but in 1910 her real name was used and became known to the public. She was also the first star to feature in a publicity stunt and to be given a contract. She made more than three hundred films, dozens of which were directed by D. W. Griffith. Tragically, in 1914 her face was burned during filming, and the scars prevented her from obtaining work. A forgotten figure, she killed herself by swallowing ant paste mixed with cough syrup at her home at 532 Westbourne.

The tomb of Cecil B. DeMille.

The grave of Florence Lawrence.

Just opposite the Cathedral Mausoleum is the marble monument of Harry Cohn (1891–1958), the founder of Columbia Pictures and one of the great movie moguls. He picked this spot so that he could see his beloved studio next door! Nearby is the bench monument for Fay Wray (1907–2004), star of the original *King Kong* (1933).

The most striking and certainly the most beautiful tomb in the cemetery is that of Douglas Fairbanks (1883–1939), the first king of Hollywood. Designed by his last wife, Lady Sylvia Ashley, it comprises a marble sarcophagus between columns at the end of a reflecting pool. There is a bronze bas-relief of his head in profile on the front, and—as with Tyrone Power—the epitaph "Good night sweet prince . . . " from the *Hamlet* soliloquy. It is said that in his will, Fairbanks left his money to be divided equally between his son Douglas Jr. (1909–2000) and Ashley once funeral costs were taken care of—so Ashley spent everything on this lavish tomb, thus ensuring that Douglas would inherit nothing. In a way, Douglas Jr. had the last laugh because, at his death, he joined his father in this tomb, and the epitaph was altered to read "sweet princes." Oddly, the grassy area next to the Fairbanks tomb has recently received a megalithic stone circle, a fitting memorial, perhaps, to Hollywood's first king!

The Cathedral Mausoleum contains numerous celebrities in addition to Rudolph Valentino, including the remains of Harvey Henderson Wilcox (1832–1891) and his wife Daeida (1861–1914). Numerous stars are there as well, both from the silent age (notably Barbara LaMarr [1896–1926], known as the "Girl Who Was Too Beautiful") and from later years, such as Peter Lorre (1904–1964), Eleanor Powell (1912–1982), and Peter Finch (1916–1977).

A mausoleum at the other end of the cemetery, the Abbey of the Psalms, also houses a number of great figures from

The tomb of Hollywood's first "king," Douglas Fairbanks.

Hollywood history: Jesse Lasky (1880–1958), the pioneer producer; the Talmadge sisters Norma (1894–1957), Constance (1898–1973), and Natalie (1896–1969); Renee Adoree (1898–1933); and Victor Fleming (1889–1949), director of *The Wizard of Oz* and *Gone with the Wind.*

Graphic artist Carl Morgan Bigsby (1898–1959) has a spectacular monument in the shape of the Pioneer Atlas missile, so he is known as the "Rocket Man"—what would an archaeologist make of this?

PLACES THEY WOULDN'T
BE SEEN DEAD IN: FOREST LAWN

Hollywood often seems to have more respect for the dead than for the living; but in some places, most notably Forest Lawn, this goes right over the top: as Oliver Hardy said, "I am willing to be buried anywhere but Forest Lawn."

Forest Lawn, Glendale (1712 South Glendale Avenue), known as "The Disneyland of the Dead," was the main inspiration of Tony Richardson's *The Loved One*, and it is one of Southern California's greatest tourist attractions. It was a traditional cemetery from its beginnings in 1906 until businessman Hubert Eaton in 1917 had a vision of a "Memorial Park" with flat markers and rolling lawns. He felt that cemeteries should inspire the living and be a celebration of life. He wanted to make "a great park, devoid of misshapen monuments and other customary signs of earthly death, but filled with towering trees, sweeping lawns, splashing fountains, singing birds, beautiful statuary, cheerful flowers, noble memorial architecture with interiors full of light and color, and redolent of the world's best history and romances." This is why Forest Lawn has no rows of tombstones, but acres of lawns, gardens, and courts. This was a new concept of a cemetery meant to attract visitors with beautiful vistas and works of art on display.

Forest Lawn is now a three-hundred-acre cemetery with over 300,000 residents. Its entrance gates, twenty-five feet high, are said to be the largest wrought-iron gates in the world. In 1934 Eaton included the first mortuary within a cemetery, as well as a coffin salesroom, crematorium, church, florist shop, and even a museum. His "Builder's Creed," from which the above quotation comes, is inscribed in stone both here and at Forest Lawn, Hollywood Hills (see below). There are full-size copies of English and Scottish churches. The Wee Kirk o' the Heather, where Ronald Reagan married Jane Wyman on January 6, 1940, is a copy of a church in Glencairn, Scotland, where Annie Laurie worshipped. The Church of the Recessional is a replica of Rudyard Kipling's home church in Rottingdean, England. And the Little Church of the Flowers is a copy of the church in Stoke Poges where the eighteenth-century poet Thomas Gray wrote his "Elegy Written in a Country Churchyard."

The Hall of the Crucifixion-Resurrection displays two huge paintings: *The Crucifixion*, an 1897 production by Polish artist Jan Styka, which is 195 feet long and 45 feet high and thought to be the world's biggest framed and mounted canvas; and the more modest *The Resurrection* (1965) by American artist Robert Clark, which is merely 70 feet long and 51 feet high.

There are even copies of Michelangelo's most famous statues, in Carrara marble—though the first huge *David* fell victim to an earthquake and had to be replaced—and a replica of the doors of Florence's Baptistry of St. John. The museum also contains an amazing range of material from medieval stained glass to suits of armor and even a small Easter Island stone head. How would our alien archaeologist of the future explain such a museum in the middle of a huge cemetery?

Forest Lawn, Glendale, has two mausolea, one of which, the Great Mausoleum, is as grand as a medieval cathedral (it has even been called "the New World's Westminster Abbey"). It contains a large number of major stars. In the accessible areas there are Jean Harlow, Clark Gable and Carole Lombard, Irving Thalberg, David Selznick, and, most recently, Elizabeth Taylor. In the inaccessible, locked section are other major figures including Harold Lloyd, W. C. Fields, and Wallace Reid. The ground floor of the Great Mausoleum contains a huge stained-glass version of da Vinci's *Last Supper*, in front of which is the Memorial Court of Honor containing reproductions of Michelangelo statues such as the *Pietá* and figures from Florence's Medici Chapel.

Elsewhere in the cemetery, the Court of Freedom contains a statue of George Washington and a seven-link section of the great chain (originally 1,800 feet long) which was strung across New York's Hudson River to keep British warships from attacking the river's forts. Each link weighs 350 pounds. It also has a huge mosaic reproduction of John Trumbull's famous painting *Declaration of Independence.* Down the hill is a full-size copy of a thirteenth-century labyrinth from the floor of Chartres cathedral in France.

Inside the nearby Freedom Mausoleum is a further collection of celebrities, including Chico Marx, Francis X. Bushman, and Billie Dove. One particular section contains Clara Bow, Alan Ladd (with a small bust in front), Jeannette McDonald, George Burns, and Nat King Cole. Outside the Freedom Mausoleum are Walt Disney, Errol Flynn, Spencer Tracy, and Clayton Moore. There are also locked gardens within the cemetery housing such major figures as Mary Pickford and Humphrey Bogart.

The area's other major Forest Lawn cemetery, in Hollywood Hills (at 6300 Forest Lawn Drive, Burbank), was built on the hillside where, in 1915, D. W. Griffith shot most of the battle sequences for *The Birth of a Nation.* Hubert Eaton, the founder of Forest Lawn, Glendale, bought this area in 1944 and opened it as a 450-acre cemetery in 1948. Whereas Glendale's basic theme

The tomb of Hollywood's first "queen," Mary Pickford.

is religion, that of Hollywood Hills is American history. It contains statues of Washington and Lincoln, as well as full-size replicas of Boston's Old North Church and Longfellow's Church of the Hills meetinghouse in New England. It also features "the largest historical mosaic in the world," a composite in glass of twenty-five famous paintings of notable events in American history. And somewhat incongruously, there is also the Plaza of Mesoamerican Heritage, containing full-size replicas of famous stone sculptures from the Olmec, Mayan, and Aztec cultures. Any archaeologist of the future would surely be baffled as to why presidential statues as well as these antiquities would be present inside this huge cemetery!

As for graves, this Forest Lawn contains some truly major Hollywood figures, most notably Buster Keaton and Stan Laurel, in close proximity to each other, as well as Bette Davis, Tex Avery, Fritz Lang, Snub Pollard, and Gene Autry. It is a really beautiful park, with views of the Burbank studios, including those of Walt Disney.

PLACES THEY WERE DYING TO END UP IN: THE OTHER CEMETERIES

There is a wide variety of other important cemeteries, each containing a variety of major figures. For example, Westwood Village Memorial Park (at 1218 Glendon Avenue), despite its tiny size (less than three acres), is now reckoned to be the most expensive in the world. Founded in 1904 and now hidden among high-rise buildings, it is located close to the University of California, Los Angeles, and Rodeo Drive, and it is absolutely packed with celebrities. It is reckoned that, currently, a small niche for an urn costs around $25,000, while a two-grave plot with a garden is $500,000. Some graves remain unmarked because the families of the deceased have not yet paid the bill—it is thought that this is why the remains of Peter Lawford were removed, cremated, and scattered at sea. On the other hand, some other stars in this cemetery—George C. Scott, Frank Zappa, Roy Orbison—are unmarked through choice.

By far the most notable grave here is Marilyn Monroe's wall crypt in the Corridor of Memories, which undergoes such a wide variety of attentions that it presents an interesting anthropological study. Her ex-husband Joe DiMaggio had six red roses placed on her crypt three times a week for twenty years until 1982. Even today there are always flowers, and sometimes cards. Some years ago, lipstick kisses started appearing, and attempts to clean them off have caused the cement to become brown. On my most recent visit in 2013, there were numerous lipstick kisses, and a new fad had begun of placing coins on the metal name-plaque. It is said that the empty crypt beside hers was bought for $25,000 by Hugh Hefner so that he could spend eternity next to the woman whose photos helped launch *Playboy* magazine's empire. The man buried above her, Richard Poncher, had his coffin inserted upside down so that he does not have his back to Marilyn. Only in Hollywood!

The placing of pennies on Natalie Wood's grave began in the 1990s—nobody knows why. Among the many other notable graves here are those of Burt Lancaster, Jack Lemmon, Billy

Marilyn Monroe's grave with kisses from fans, which began to appear around 1996.

Wilder, Walter Matthau, Dean Martin, and James Coburn. Archaeologists will be particularly intrigued by the plaque for Richard Conte, which has a pyramid in each corner, and a question mark after the year of his death!

Holy Cross cemetery (at 5835 West Slauson Avenue), founded in 1939, is the region's principal Catholic burial ground, and its two hundred acres feature some notable silent-era stars, most notably Mack Sennett. Among the many other celebrities are Bing Crosby, Mario Lanza, Jimmy Durante, and Mary Astor. Bela Lugosi's funeral was paid for by Frank Sinatra—he lay in state at Strothers Mortuary (southeast Hollywood Boulevard and Argyle) in his high-collared Dracula cape.

One intriguing story concerns Gary Cooper (1901–1961). After his funeral at the Church of the Good Shepherd, he was buried in the small "Lourdes grotto" in Holy Cross. Thirteen years later, his widow decided to marry a doctor in New England, and she therefore had Gary disinterred and took him with her, reburying him in the Sacred Heart Cemetery at Southampton, Long Island, under a three-ton boulder. When her new husband died, she buried him in a more modest grave beside Gary, and she is then said to have returned to California, leaving the two husbands together for eternity! Cooper's old plot in the Lourdes grotto is now occupied by Rita Hayworth.

Not far away, Hillside Memorial Park and Mortuary (at 6001 Centinela Avenue) was created in 1942 as a last resting place for the Jewish community of southern California. It contains Hollywood's most spectacular tomb by far. Al Jolson (1886–1950) died of a heart attack at sixty-four, and he was first buried at Beth Olam Cemetery in Hollywood, where twenty thousand people attended his funeral. His widow Erle was unhappy because that cemetery would not allow her to build what she considered a suitable memorial to him. The owners of Hillside then approached her and assured her that she could build such a memorial in their park. Eleven months later, Jolson had a second funeral and an interment in the largest and most impressive tomb in Hollywood. It is said that his widow paid $9,000 for

Hollywood's most spectacular tomb, that of Al Jolson in Hillside.

the plot, and $75,000 for the monument. The elegant domed, columned, hillside memorial rises above a 120-foot, blue-tiled cascade of water. A three-quarter-size statue of Jolson, on one knee, arms outstretched, presumably singing "Mammy," is close to the great sarcophagus (Jolson is the only star with an effigy of himself next to his tomb, except for Alan Ladd who, as mentioned above, has a bust). The six pillars around the sarcophagus rise to the great dome, on the underside of which is a mosaic of Moses with the Ten Commandments, and the words "The Sweet Singer of Israel." It is said that Jolson wanted a modest grave near a waterfall; but his widow had other ideas. What was created, therefore was a permanent reminder to the world that he was considered—and considered himself—"the greatest entertainer the world has ever seen."

Other cemeteries—Inglewood, Rosedale, Valhalla, Grandview, Oakwood, Woodlawn, San Fernando Mission, Home of Peace, Calvary, Eden, Mount Sinai—contain far fewer major stars, but each has its interesting graves, which are listed in the appendix. These cemetery celebrity lists are in no way exhaustive but instead focus on people I find important or interesting. Fuller lists for a few of the cemeteries can be found in some of the books in the bibliography.

PAMPERED PETS: THE ANIMAL CEMETERIES

Finally, our alien archaeologists of the future will occasionally encounter burials of animals, which may well cause some puzzlement. Hollywood often cared greatly for its departed animals.

It is rumored that Tom Mix's first horse, Old Blue, was buried at "Mixville," a Western town built at 2450 Glendale where Mix made his films. The grave is now under the parking lot of a bank (2496 Glendale), and one wonders how archaeologists would interpret a horse skeleton at this site!

William S. Hart, the first cowboy star in silent movies, bequeathed his 250-acre ranch to be used as a public park on his death. The estate, at 24151 Newhall Avenue, in Newhall in the San Fernando Valley, also contains the cemetery of his eleven beloved dogs (mostly Great Danes) and a special enclosure for the impressive tomb of his favorite pinto pony, Fritz (1907–1938), bearing a bas-relief bronze portrait and the inscription "A loyal comrade."

The Pet Memorial Park at 5068 North Old Scandia Lane, Calabasas, contains numerous animals which have been buried in these ten acres since it was founded in 1928. They include Hopalong Cassidy's horse, Topper; Chief and Mrs. Thunder

The graves of William S. Hart's dogs.

The grave of William S. Hart's pony, Fritz.

Cloud's horses, Smoke and Sunny, "famous horses of stage and screen"; Lauren Bacall's dog, Droopy; and Lionel Barrymore's cat, Pukie. But doubtless the most noteworthy occupant is Kabar, who was a black Doberman, and the best loved of Rudolph Valentino's dozen dogs. He died three years after his master, "of a broken heart" according to Valentino's nephew.

Archaeologists of the future will find it extremely difficult to comprehend the Hollywood cemeteries, which range from small to enormous and whose contents encompass a vast variety from innumerable modest flat plaques and unmarked graves to tombstones, obelisks, Greco-Roman temples, and mausolea. They might reasonably interpret the big monuments as indicative of great wealth, but the many modest markers for equally prominent stars would go unnoticed. And if they were unable

Hopalong Cassidy's horse, Topper, in the Pet Memorial Park.

The grave of Kabar, Valentino's beloved Doberman.

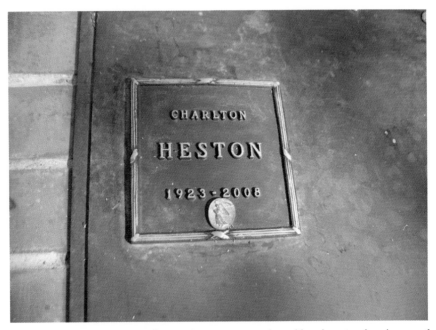

Some of the graves in Hollywood are very modest, like the simple plaque of Charlton Heston.

to read the explicit tributes on a handful of graves, they would have no clue whatsoever as to the source of the fame and fortune of the deceased—let alone any clue to the reasons for the buried animals!

In addition to the books listed in the bibliography, readers interested in Hollywood cemeteries are advised to consult www .beneathlosangeles.com and www.seeing-stars.com. In addition, "Hollywood Underground" is a group of aficionados who seek out graves and sometimes raise funds to place markers, such as on the grave of Alan Crosland, an early director (he directed the first talkie, *The Jazz Singer*, in 1927) in Hollywood Memorial Park (see www.hollywood-underground.com).

Conclusion

Twilight of the Gods

"Hollywood," a seemingly innocuous word, eventually became three magical syllables which denoted the "Capital of Kitsch"—the world's most glamorous company town, a kingdom of conspicuous consumption, a dream factory churning out endless escapist entertainment that invoked a wonderful world of make-believe. It has often been called Tinseltown, and indeed, in the words of Oscar Levant, "Strip away the phony tinsel of Hollywood and you find the real tinsel underneath."

Hollywood's products induced the faithful—people of all kinds and from all over the world—to come and worship in massive picture palaces accompanied by music, paying homage to their favorite stars, a whole series of kings and queens, or indeed new gods and goddesses. These picture palaces were often lavish and awe-inspiring settings for magical experiences and rituals, for gazing at make-believe mirages. Hollywood had created the most powerful cultural influence the world had ever seen, using the universal language of mime, what has been called

"Esperanto for the eyes." The public rapidly developed an insatiable appetite for movies.

And inevitably the sudden influx of untold wealth had all kinds of repercussions, not only for the businessmen who controlled the "Hollywood Culture" but also and especially for the often very ordinary people who were catapulted to world fame and adoration. As Anita Loos said of the phenomenon in the 1920s, "To place in the limelight a great number of people who ordinarily would be chambermaids and chauffeurs, and give them unlimited power and wealth, is bound to produce lively results." Roscoe "Fatty" Arbuckle, for example, had been a plumber's assistant but he swiftly became a multimillionaire. Hollywood rapidly began to emulate the decadence of the Roman empire, or the land of the lotus-eaters, peopled by drug-crazed, alcoholic, sex-mad libertines with vast wealth and often little good taste. The inevitable result was a never-ending series of scandals and tragedies.

And yet . . . this incredibly powerful culture, this all-conquering industry, has left very little in the way of material remains which might tell the archaeologists of the future exactly what occurred here. As we have seen from chapter to chapter, if these archaeologists had no prior knowledge of this culture, they simply could not deduce anything much about the movie industry or the movie-star phenomenon from the few surviving clues scattered here and there over a huge area. As shown throughout this book, Hollywood contains a bizarre mixture of styles—Egyptian, Chinese, Babylonian, Italian, Spanish, Mayan, Moorish, Tudor, Greco-Roman, Art Deco, and even Hansel-and-Gretel. Imagine an archaeologist encountering the Getty Museum's Roman villa in this region; or even more bizarrely, encountering the contents of Disneyland: a medieval-style castle, statues of elephants with huge ears, giant teacups and saucers, a spooky mansion, a snowy mountain, statues of elephants and hippos along and in waterways . . .

The Hollywood stars are indeed like stars in that their light is still reaching us on movie screens after they themselves have long gone out. Death is no longer absolute; they have cheated the void. With the wonders of modern technology and computer-generated imagery, it is even possible now to make new movies featuring long-dead stars. But the place where the magic was created has been more effectively destroyed. It is my hope that this offbeat but wide-ranging tour of the surviving traces of the "Hollywood Culture" will help stimulate more people to take an interest in, to seek out, and to help preserve and mark those relics for posterity before it is too late.

For example, 80 percent of silent films have already perished. One of the greatest tragedies of the movie industry is the studios' lack of interest in their past products—over the decades, the majority of their silent output has been lost to fires (early film was extremely inflammable), decomposition, and neglect. Many hundreds of films, probably thousands, have been destroyed or lost. Some continue to turn up in private collections, foreign film libraries and archives, and trunks in attics, cellars, and garages. Fortunately, there are devotees dedicated to the rediscovery and preservation of this irreplaceable heritage—groups such as the Silent Comedy Mafia, a loose organization of scholars, historians, and archivists who seek out lost films by early comedians (www.silentcomedymafia.com).

Throughout the twentieth century, the city officials of the Los Angeles area always favored growth over historic preservation. For example, there was constant friction between those who saw Hollywood Boulevard as a national treasure and those who always wanted new development. Consequently Los Angeles—like Hollywood itself—has been called "the town without a memory" and "a city that is really famous for the disregard of its own past."

There are now organizations devoted to trying to save what little survives. We have already mentioned Hollywood Heritage (see introduction). In April 2009, the Getty Conservation Institute joined forces with the Los Angeles Office of Historic Resources and the Library Foundation of Los Angeles to carry out a systematic survey to identify the city's surviving historic resources. This search for the hidden gems of the history and architecture of Los Angeles is seen as a major step forward for the historic preservation movement; indeed, the Los Angeles Conservancy is now the largest membership-based local historic preservation organization in the United States (www.laconser vancy.org; see also www.myhistoricla.org and http://preserva tion.lacity.org).

It is perhaps too little, too late, but one hopes that these organizations will indeed manage to save the few surviving relics of that golden age when the "Hollywood Culture" suddenly arose out of nothing and affected the entire world.

Appendix

Lists of Resting Places

WHEREABOUTS OF CELEBRITIES IN THE LOS ANGELES AREA

Bud ABBOTT	Ashes scattered over the Pacific
Don ADAMS	Hollywood Memorial
Buddy ADLER	Forest Lawn, Glendale
Rene ADOREE	Hollywood Memorial
Iris ADRIAN	Forest Lawn, Hollywood Hills
Eddie ALBERT	Westwood
Robert ALDA	Forest Lawn, Glendale
Gracie ALLEN	Forest Lawn, Glendale
Irwin ALLEN	Mount Sinai
June ALLYSON	Ashes returned to family
Robert ALTMAN	Ashes returned to family
Don AMECHE	Ashes returned to family
Leon AMES	Forest Lawn, Hollywood Hills
Morey AMSTERDAM	Forest Lawn, Hollywood Hills
Eddie "Rochester" ANDERSON	Evergreen Cemetery, Los Angeles

Dana ANDREWS	Ashes returned to family
Laverne and Maxine ANDREWS (Sisters)	Forest Lawn, Glendale
Minta Durfee ARBUCKLE	Forest Lawn, Glendale
Roscoe "Fatty" ARBUCKLE	Ashes scattered in California
Eve ARDEN	Westwood
Richard ARLEN	Holy Cross
Desi ARNAZ	Ashes scattered at sea
James ARNESS	Forest Lawn, Glendale
Jean ARTHUR	Ashes scattered over the Pacific
Fred ASTAIRE (and Adele)	Oakwood Memorial Park, Chatsworth, Los Angeles
Mary ASTOR	Holy Cross
Lionel ATWILL	Chapel of the Pines
Gene AUTRY	Forest Lawn, Hollywood Hills
Frederick B. "Tex" AVERY	Forest Lawn, Hollywood Hills
Agnes AYRES	Hollywood Memorial
Lew AYRES	Westwood
Jim BACKUS	Westwood
Vilma BANKY	Ashes scattered over the Pacific
Theda BARA	Forest Lawn, Glendale
Joseph BARBERA	Forest lawn, Glendale
Binnie BARNES	Forest Lawn, Glendale
Gene BARRY	Hillside
Ethel BARRYMORE	Calvary
John BARRYMORE	Was at Calvary; now in Philadelphia
Lionel BARRYMORE	Calvary
Richard BASEHART	Westwood
L. Frank BAUM	Forest Lawn, Glendale
Warner BAXTER	Forest Lawn, Glendale
Noah BEERY Jr.	Forest Lawn, Hollywood Hills
Noah BEERY Sr.	Forest Lawn, Hollywood Hills
Wallace BEERY	Forest Lawn, Glendale

Ed BEGLEY	San Fernando Mission
Ralph BELLAMY	Forest Lawn, Hollywood Hills
Bea BENADARET	Valhalla
William BENDIX	San Fernando Mission
Jack BENNY (and his wife Mary)	Hillside
Edgar BERGEN	Inglewood
Milton BERLE	Hillside
Paul BERN	Inglewood
Mel BLANC	Hollywood Memorial Park
Clara BLANDICK	Forest Lawn, Glendale
Joan BLONDELL	Forest Lawn, Glendale
Eric BLORE	Forest Lawn, Glendale
Ben BLUE	Hillside
Betty BLYTHE	Forest Lawn, Glendale
Humphrey BOGART	Forest Lawn, Glendale
John BOLES	Westwood
Ray BOLGER	Holy Cross
Gutzon BORGLUM	Forest Lawn, Glendale
Ernest BORGNINE	Ashes returned to family
Clara BOW	Forest Lawn, Glendale
Stephen BOYD	Oakwood Memorial Park, Chatsworth, Los Angeles
William BOYD	Forest Lawn, Glendale
Charles BOYER	Holy Cross
Peter BOYLE	Ashes returned to family
Ray BRADBURY	Westwood
Scott BRADY	Holy Cross
Marlon BRANDO	Ashes scattered in Death Valley
Keefe BRASSELLE (John D. Brasselli)	Holy Cross
Eileen BRENNAN	Ashes returned to family
Walter BRENNAN	San Fernando Mission
Fanny BRICE	Westwood
Lloyd BRIDGES	Ashes scattered at sea
Richard BRIGHT	Ashes returned to family

Albert "Cubby" BROCCOLI	Forest Lawn, Hollywood Hills
Rand BROOKS	Forest Lawn, Glendale
Clarence BROWN	Forest Lawn, Glendale
Jim BROWN	Ashes scattered at sea
Joe E. BROWN	Forest Lawn, Glendale
Les BROWN (bandleader)	Westwood
Coral BROWNE	Hollywood Memorial Park
Lenny BRUCE (Schneider)	Eden, Mission Hills
Nigel BRUCE	Chapel of the Pines
George BURNS	Forest Lawn, Glendale
Edgar Rice BURROUGHS	Under tree, 18354 Ventura Boulevard, Tarzana, Los Angeles
Mae BUSCH	Chapel of the Pines
Francis X. BUSHMAN	Forest Lawn, Glendale
Red BUTTONS	Ashes returned to family
Sebastian CABOT	Westwood
Sammy CAHN	Westwood
Louis CALHERN	Hollywood Memorial
Rory CALHOUN	Ashes returned to family
Godfrey CAMBRIDGE	Forest Lawn, Hollywood Hills
Eric CAMPBELL	Rosedale
John CANDY	Holy Cross
Eddie CANTOR	Hillside
Yakima CANUTT	Valhalla
Truman CAPOTE	Westwood
MacDonald CAREY	Holy Cross
Yvonne de CARLO	Ashes returned to family
Karen CARPENTER	Was in Forest Lawn, Cypress; now in family mausoleum at Valley Oaks Memorial Park, Westlake Village, California
David CARRADINE	Forest Lawn, Hollywood Hills

John CARRADINE	Body buried at sea between California and Catalina
Leo G. CARROLL	Grandview Cemetery, Glendale
Jack CARSON	Forest Lawn, Glendale
Johnny CARSON	Ashes returned to family
Adriana CASELOTTI (*Snow White*)	Ashes scattered off Newport Beach
John CASSAVETES	Westwood
Jeff CHANDLER (Ira Grossel)	Hillside
Lon CHANEY Jr.	Body donated to University of Southern California School of Medicine
Lon CHANEY Sr.	Forest Lawn, Glendale
Hannah CHAPLIN (Charlie Chaplin's mother)	Hollywood Memorial
Norman Spencer CHAPLIN	Inglewood
Marguerite CHAPMAN	Holy Cross
Cyd CHARISSE	Hillside
Ray CHARLES	Inglewood
Charley CHASE (Parrott)	Forest Lawn, Glendale
Mae CLARKE	Valhalla
Lana CLARKSON (death at Phil Spector's house)	Hollywood Memorial
Jill CLAYBURGH	Ashes returned to family
Lee J. COBB	Mount Sinai
James COBURN	Westwood
Eddie COCHRAN	Forest Lawn, Cypress
Iron Eyes CODY	Hollywood Memorial
Harry COHN	Hollywood Memorial
Nat King COLE	Forest Lawn, Glendale
Ray COLLINS	Forest Lawn, Hollywood Hills
Jerry COLONNA	San Fernando Mission
Russ COLUMBO	Forest Lawn, Glendale
Chester CONKLIN	Ashes scattered at sea

Ray CONNIFF	Westwood
Chuck CONNORS	San Fernando Mission
William CONRAD	Forest Lawn, Hollywood Hills
Richard CONTE	Westwood
Tom CONWAY	Chapel of the Pines
Jackie COOGAN (John Leslie)	Holy Cross
Elisha COOK Jr.	Ashes scattered in mountains near Bishop, California
Sam COOKE	Forest Lawn, Glendale
Gary COOPER	Was at Holy Cross; now in Long Island, New York
Carmine COPPOLA	San Fernando Mission Cemetery
Lou COSTELLO (Cristillo)	Calvary
Bob CRANE	Westwood
Norma CRANE	Westwood
CRISWELL	Valhalla
Bing CROSBY	Holy Cross
Alan CROSLAND	Hollywood Memorial
Benjamin S. "Scatman" CROTHERS	Forest Lawn, Hollywood Hills
George CUKOR	Forest Lawn, Glendale
Constance CUMMINGS	Ashes returned to family and friends
Robert CUMMINGS	Forest Lawn, Glendale
Michael CURTIZ	Forest Lawn, Glendale
Viola DANA	Hollywood Memorial
Dorothy DANDRIDGE	Forest Lawn, Glendale
Rodney DANGERFIELD	Westwood
Henry DANIELL	Woodlawn, Santa Monica
Bebe DANIELS	Hollywood Memorial
Bobby DARIN	Body left to medicine
Jane DARWELL (Patti Woodard)	Forest Lawn, Glendale
Joe DASSIN	Hollywood Memorial

Marion DAVIES (Douras)	Hollywood Memorial
Bette DAVIS	Forest Lawn, Hollywood Hills
Brad DAVIS	Forest Lawn, Hollywood Hills
Jim DAVIS	Forest Lawn, Glendale
Joan DAVIS	Holy Cross
Sammy DAVIS Jr.	Forest Lawn, Glendale
Sandra DEE	Forest Lawn, Hollywood Hills
Dom DELUISE	Ashes returned to family
William DEMAREST	Forest Lawn, Glendale
Cecil B. DEMILLE	Hollywood Memorial
John DEREK	Ashes returned to family
Joe DeRITA (3 Stooges)	Valhalla
Roy DISNEY (brother)	Forest Lawn, Hollywood Hills
Roy DISNEY (nephew)	Ashes scattered at sea
Walt DISNEY	Forest Lawn, Glendale
DOLLY SISTERS	Forest Lawn, Glendale
Brian DONLEVY	Ashes scattered at sea
Billie DOVE	Forest Lawn, Glendale
Marie DRESSLER	Forest Lawn, Glendale
Paulette DUBOST	Ashes returned to family
Margaret DUMONT	Chapel of the Pines
Michael Clarke DUNCAN	Forest Lawn, Hollywood Hills
Dominique DUNNE	Westwood
Irene DUNNE	Calvary
Jimmy DURANTE	Holy Cross
Dan DURYEA	Forest Lawn, Hollywood Hills
Buddy EBSEN	Ashes scattered at sea
Nelson EDDY	Hollywood Memorial
Blake EDWARDS	Ashes returned to family
Cliff EDWARDS	Valhalla
Richard EGAN	Holy Cross
Jack ELAM	Ashes returned to Los Angeles
Mama Cass ELLIOT	Mount Sinai
Nora EPHRON	Ashes scattered
Tom EWELL	Ashes returned to family

Max FACTOR	Hillside
Douglas FAIRBANKS Jr.	Hollywood Memorial
Douglas FAIRBANKS Sr.	Hollywood Memorial
Percy FAITH	Hillside
Peter FALK	Westwood
Richard FARNSWORTH	Forest Lawn, Hollywood Hills
Farrah FAWCETT	Westwood
Fritz FELD	Mount Sinai
Marty FELDMAN	Forest Lawn, Hollywood Hills
Stepin FETCHIT	Calvary
W. C. FIELDS	Forest Lawn, Glendale
Peter FINCH	Hollywood Memorial
Larry FINE (3 Stooges)	Forest Lawn, Glendale
James FINLAYSON	Chapel of the Pines
Ella FITZGERALD	Inglewood
Victor FLEMING	Hollywood Memorial
Jay C. FLIPPEN	Westwood
Errol FLYNN	Forest Lawn, Glendale
Joe FLYNN	Holy Cross
Henry FONDA	Ashes kept by family in Bel Air house
Glenn FORD	Woodlawn
John FORD	Holy Cross
Tony FRANCIOSA	Ashes returned to family
Anne FRANCIS	Ashes returned to family
James FRANCISCUS	Ashes returned to family
John FRANKENHEIMER	Ashes returned to family
William FRAWLEY	San Fernando Mission
Arthur FREED	Hillside
Kathleen FREEMAN	Hollywood Memorial
Friz FRELENG	Hillside
Rudolf FRIML	Forest Lawn, Glendale
Clark GABLE	Forest Lawn, Glendale
Eva GABOR	Westwood
Reginald GARDINER	Forest Lawn, Hollywood Hills
Anita GARVIN	San Fernando Mission
Marvin GAYE	Ashes scattered at sea

Janet GAYNOR (Gregory)	Hollywood Memorial (next to Adrian)
J. Paul GETTY	Mausoleum behind Getty Museum, Malibu, California
Alice GHOSTLEY	Ashes returned to family
Andy GIBB	Forest Lawn, Hollywood Hills
Hoot GIBSON	Inglewood
John GILBERT	Forest Lawn, Glendale
Hermione GINGOLD	Forest Lawn, Glendale
Paul GLEASON	Westwood
Alexander GODUNOV	Ashes distributed between two girlfriends
Jerry GOLDSMITH	Hillside
Samuel GOLDWYN	Forest Lawn, Glendale
Gale GORDON	Ashes scattered at sea
Robert GOULET	Ashes returned to family
Betty GRABLE	Inglewood
Stewart GRANGER	Ashes returned to Malibu home
Cary GRANT	Ashes scattered over the Pacific
Sid GRAUMAN	Forest Lawn, Glendale
Peter GRAVES	Ashes returned to family
Kathryn GRAYSON	Ashes returned to family
Lorne GREENE	Hillside
Sydney GREENSTREET	Forest Lawn, Glendale
Lita GREY (Chaplin)	Hollywood Memorial
Edmund GWENN	Chapel of the Pines
Buddy HACKETT	Hillside
Joan HACKETT	Hollywood Memorial
Larry HAGMAN	Ashes scattered
William HAINES	Woodlawn, Santa Monica, California
Jack HALEY	Holy Cross
Oliver HARDY	Valhalla
Mickey HARGITAY	Ashes returned to family
Jean HARLOW	Forest Lawn, Glendale
Mildred HARRIS	Hollywood Memorial
T. Marvin HATLEY	Forest Lawn, Hollywood Hills
June HAVER	Holy Cross

George "Gabby" HAYES	Forest Lawn, Hollywood Hills
Rita HAYWORTH	Holy Cross
Edith HEAD	Forest Lawn, Glendale
Van HEFLIN	Ashes scattered over the Pacific
Percy HELTON	Westwood
Paul HENREID	Woodlawn, Santa Monica, California
Jean HERSHOLT	Forest Lawn, Glendale
Charlton HESTON	Urn garden, St. Matthew's Episcopal Church Columbarium, Pacific Palisades, Los Angeles County
Pat HINGLE	Ashes scattered at sea
Alfred HITCHCOCK	Ashes scattered at sea
John HODIAK	Calvary
William HOLDEN	Ashes scattered over the Pacific
Sterling HOLLOWAY	Ashes scattered over the Pacific
Celeste HOLM	Ashes returned to family
Bob HOPE	San Fernando Mission Cemetery
Edward Everett HORTON	Forest Lawn, Glendale
John HOUSEMAN	Ashes scattered
Jerome "Curly" HOWARD (3 Stooges)	Home of Peace
Moe HOWARD (3 Stooges)	Hillside Memorial Park
Shemp HOWARD (3 Stooges)	Home of Peace
Rock HUDSON	Ashes scattered over the Pacific
John HUSTON	Hollywood Memorial
Rex INGRAM	Forest Lawn, Hollywood Hills
Jill IRELAND	Ashes scattered in front of Malibu home or in Charles Bronson's walking stick
Christopher ISHERWOOD	Body donated to University of California, Los Angeles, Medical Center
Jose ITURBI	Holy Cross
Michael JACKSON	Forest Lawn, Glendale

David JANSSEN	Hillside
George JESSEL	Hillside
Nunnally JOHNSON	Westwood
Van JOHNSON	Ashes returned to family
Al JOLSON	Hillside
Carolyn JONES	Melrose Abbey, Anaheim, California
Chuck JONES	Ashes scattered at sea
Jennifer JONES	Forest Lawn, Glendale
Spike JONES	Holy Cross
Jim and Marian JORDAN	Holy Cross
Louis JOURDAN	Westwood
Gus KAHN	Forest Lawn, Glendale
Bob KANE	Forest Lawn, Hollywood Hills
Terry Allen KATH	Forest Lawn, Glendale
Buster KEATON	Forest Lawn, Hollywood Hills
Brian KEITH	Westwood
DeForest KELLEY	Ashes scatted at sea
Gene KELLY	Ashes returned to family
Edgar KENNEDY	Holy Cross
Barbara KENT	Ashes scattered at sea
Stan KENTON	Westwood
Ward KIMBALL	Ashes returned to family
Klaus KINSKI	Ashes scattered over the Pacific
Bruno KIRBY	Ashes returned to family
Jack KLUGMAN	Ashes returned to family
Ted KNIGHT	Forest Lawn, Glendale
Don KNOTTS	Westwood
Harvey KORMAN	Woodlawn
Ernie KOVACS	Forest Lawn, Hollywood Hills
Alan LADD	Forest Lawn, Glendale
Carl LAEMMLE	Home of Peace
Don LAFONTAINE	Hollywood Memorial
Barbara LA MARR	Hollywood Memorial
Fernando LAMAS	Ashes scattered over the Pacific
Dorothy LAMOUR	Forest Lawn, Hollywood Hills
Louis L'AMOUR	Forest Lawn, Glendale

Burt LANCASTER	Westwood
Elsa LANCHESTER	Ashes scattered over the Pacific
Carole LANDIS	Forest Lawn, Glendale
Michael LANDON	Hillside
Fritz LANG	Forest Lawn, Hollywood Hills
Harry LANGDON	Grandview Cemetery, Glendale
Walter LANTZ (Woody Woodpecker)	Forest Lawn, Hollywood Hills
Mario LANZA	Holy Cross
Jesse LASKY	Hollywood Memorial
Charles LAUGHTON	Forest Lawn, Hollywood Hills
Stan LAUREL	Forest Lawn, Hollywood Hills
Lucille LAVERNE (the queen in *Snow White*)	Inglewood
John Philip LAW	Ashes scattered at sea
Peter LAWFORD	Ashes scattered over the Pacific
Florence LAWRENCE	Hollywood Memorial
Marc LAWRENCE	Ashes returned to family and friends
Irving "Swifty" LAZAR	Westwood
Dixie LEE (Crosby)	Holy Cross
Gypsy Rose LEE	Inglewood
Peggy LEE	Westwood
Henry LEHRMAN	Hollywood Memorial
Jerry LEIBER	Hillside
Janet LEIGH	Ashes returned to family
Harvey LEMBECK (Cpl. Barbella in "Bilko")	Eden, Mission Hills
Jack LEMMON	Westwood
Oscar LEVANT	Westwood
Al LEWIS	Ashes in favorite cigar box
Shari LEWIS	Ashes returned to family
Wladziu Valentino LIBERACE	Forest Lawn, Hollywood Hills
Elmo LINCOLN	Hollywood Memorial
Harold LLOYD	Forest Lawn, Glendale
Gene LOCKHART	Holy Cross

Carole LOMBARD	Forest Lawn, Glendale
Julie LONDON	Forest Lawn, Hollywood Hills
Peter LORRE	Hollywood Memorial
Anita LOUISE (Adler Berger)	Forest Lawn, Glendale
Frank LOVEJOY	Holy Cross
Ernst LUBITSCH	Forest Lawn, Glendale
Bela LUGOSI	Holy Cross
William LUNDIGAN	Holy Cross
Ida LUPINO	Forest Lawn, Glendale
Ben LYON	Hollywood Memorial
Jeanette MACDONALD	Forest Lawn, Glendale
Mary MACLAREN	Forest Lawn, Glendale
Fred MacMURRAY	Holy Cross
Marjorie MAIN	Forest Lawn, Hollywood Hills
Karl MALDEN	Westwood
Jayne MANSFIELD (marker)	Hollywood Memorial
Janet MARGOLIN	Westwood
Kenneth MARS	Ashes returned to family
Dean MARTIN	Westwood
Dick MARTIN	Ashes scattered at sea
Quinn MARTIN	Forest Lawn, Glendale
Strother MARTIN	Forest Lawn, Hollywood Hills
Al MARTINO	Holy Cross
Chico MARX	Forest Lawn, Glendale
Groucho MARX	Eden, Mission Hills
Gummo MARX	Forest Lawn, Glendale
Zeppo MARX	Ashes scattered over the Pacific
June MATHIS	Hollywood Memorial
Walter MATTHAU	Westwood
Louis B. MAYER	Home of Peace
Mike MAZURKI	Forest Lawn, Glendale
Leo McCAREY	Holy Cross
Kevin McCARTHY	Ashes returned to family
Doug McCLURE	Woodlawn, Santa Monica

Hattie McDANIEL	Rosedale
Roddy McDOWALL	Ashes scattered at sea
Darren McGAVIN	Hollywood Memorial
Patrick McGOOHAN	Ashes returned to family
Bill McKINNEY	Ashes scattered at sea
Victor McLAGLEN	Forest Lawn, Glendale
Butterfly McQUEEN	Body donated to science, University of Georgia
Steve McQUEEN	Ashes scattered over the Pacific (but some with daughter Terry in Westwood)
Allan MELVIN (Bilko)	Westwood
Adolphe MENJOU	Hollywood Memorial
Burgess MEREDITH	Ashes returned to family
Lewix MILESTONE	Westwood
Ray MILLAND	Ashes scattered over the Pacific
Ann MILLER	Holy Cross
Vincent MINNELLI	Forest Lawn, Glendale
Mary Miles MINTER	Ashes scattered
Thomas MITCHELL	Chapel of the Pines
Robert MITCHUM	Ashes scattered at sea
Tom MIX	Forest Lawn, Glendale
Marilyn MONROE	Westwood
Ricardo MONTALBAN	Holy Cross
Elizabeth MONTGOMERY	Ashes returned to family
Robert MONTGOMERY	Ashes returned to family
Clayton MOORE	Forest Lawn, Glendale
Colleen MOORE (Katherine Maginot)	Ashes scattered over the Pacific
Harry MORGAN	Ashes returned to family
Anita MORRIS	Ashes returned to family
Jeff MORRIS	Westwood
Vic MORROW	Hillside
Ferdinand "Jelly Roll" MORTON	Calvary
Paul MUNI	Hollywood Memorial

Brittany MURPHY	Forest Lawn, Hollywood Hills
Mae MURRAY	Valhalla
Clarence "Ducky" NASH	San Fernando Mission
Alla NAZIMOVA	Forest Lawn, Glendale
Pola NEGRI	Calvary
Ozzie and Rick NELSON	Forest Lawn, Hollywood Hills
Paul NEWMAN	Ashes returned to family
Lloyd NOLAN	Westwood
Mabel NORMAND	Calvary
Sheree NORTH	Ashes returned to family
Ramón NOVARRO	Calvary
Maila NURMI (Vampira)	Hollywood Memorial
Edmond O'BRIEN	Holy Cross
George O'BRIEN	Buried at sea off San Diego
Pat O'BRIEN	Holy Cross
Carroll O'CONNOR (Archie Bunker)	Westwood
Heather O'ROURKE	Westwood
Jack OAKIE (Lewis Delaney Offield)	Forest Lawn, Glendale
Merle OBERON (Wolders)	Forest Lawn, Glendale
Barney OLDFIELD	Holy Cross
Roy ORBISON	Westwood
Edward "Kid" ORY	Holy Cross
Jack PALANCE	Ashes returned to family
Lilli PALMER (Thompson)	Forest Lawn, Glendale
Hermes PAN	Holy Cross
Alexander PANTAGES	Forest Lawn, Glendale
Eleanor PARKER	Ashes scattered at sea
Larry PARKS	Ashes returned to family
Louella PARSONS (Martin)	Holy Cross
Alice PEARCE ("Gladys Kravitz")	Ashes scattered at sea

Gregory PECK	Crypt below Our Lady of the Angels Cathedral, Los Angeles
Sam PECKINPAH	Ashes scattered over the Pacific
Chris PENN	Holy Cross
Anthony PERKINS	Ashes returned to family
Brock PETERS	Forest Lawn, Hollywood Hills
Jean PETERS	Holy Cross
Mary PHILBIN	Calvary
Mary PICKFORD	Forest Lawn, Glendale
Walter PIDGEON	Body given to science
ZaSu PITTS	Holy Cross
Suzanne PLESHETTE	Hillside
Sydney POLLACK	Some ashes scattered along runway at Van Nuys airport
Snub POLLARD	Forest Lawn, Hollywood Hills
Dick POWELL	Forest Lawn, Glendale
Eleanor POWELL	Hollywood Memorial
Tyrone POWER	Hollywood Memorial
Billy PRESTON	Inglewood
Marie PREVOST	Ashes returned to family
Vincent PRICE	Ashes scattered at sea
Freddie PRINZE	Forest Lawn, Hollywood Hills
Dorothy PROVINE	Ashes returned to family
Richard PRYOR	Ashes returned to family and friends
Edna PURVIANCE	Grandview Cemetery, Glendale
George RAFT	Forest Lawn, Hollywood Hills
Johnny RAMONE	Hollywood Memorial
Tony RANDALL	Ashes returned to family and friends
Virginia RAPPE	Hollywood Memorial
Aldo RAY	Ashes scattered over the Pacific
Andy RAZAF	Rosedale
Donna REED	Westwood
Christopher REEVE	Ashes returned to family
George REEVES	Pasadena Mausoleum, Mountain View Cemetery, Altadena, California
Wallace REID	Forest Lawn, Glendale

Lee REMICK	Ashes returned to family
Buddy RICH	Westwood
Nelson RIDDLE	Hollywood Memorial Park
Minnie RIPERTON	Westwood
John RITTER	Forest Lawn, Hollywood Hills
Dale ROBERTSON	Ashes returned to family
Sugar Ray ROBINSON	Inglewood
Gene RODDENBERRY	Ashes taken into space by Space Shuttle
Ginger ROGERS	Oakwood
Cesar ROMERO	Inglewood
Joe E. ROSS	Forest Lawn, Hollywood Hills
Harold ROSSON	Hollywood Memorial
Dan ROWAN	Ashes returned to family
Gilbert ROWLAND	Ashes scattered at sea
Miklos ROZSA	Forest Lawn, Hollywood Hills
Charles and Wesley RUGGLES	Forest Lawn, Glendale
Jane RUSSELL	Ashes scattered at sea
Rosalind RUSSELL (Brisson)	Holy Cross
Irene RYAN (Granny)	Woodlawn Memorial Park, Santa Monica
SABU (Dastigar)	Forest Lawn, Hollywood Hills
S. Z. SAKALL	Forest Lawn, Glendale
Turu SATANA	Ashes returned to family
George SAVALAS	Forest Lawn, Hollywood Hills
Telly SAVALAS	Forest Lawn, Hollywood Hills
Gia SCALA	Holy Cross
Roy SCHEIDER	Ashes returned to family
George C. SCOTT	Westwood
Raymond SCOTT (Looney Tunes)	Ashes returned to family
Tony SCOTT	Ashes returned to family
David O. SELZNICK and family	Forest Lawn, Glendale
Aimee SEMPLE MACPHERSON	Forest Lawn, Glendale

Mack SENNETT	Holy Cross
Dick SHAWN	Hillside
Norma SHEARER	Forest Lawn, Glendale
Ann SHERIDAN	Hollywood Memorial
Allan SHERMAN	Hillside
Robert SHERMAN	Hillside
Dinah SHORE	Hillside
Benjamin "Bugsy" SIEGEL	Hollywood Memorial
Phil SILVERS	Mount Sinai
Jean SIMMONS	Ashes scattered at family home
Red SKELTON	Forest Lawn, Glendale
Everett SLOANE	Rosedale
Bubba SMITH	Ashes returned to family
Aaron SPELLING	Hillside
Lionel STANDER	Forest Lawn, Glendale
Rod STEIGER	Forest Lawn, Hollywood Hills
Jules STEIN	Forest Lawn, Glendale
Max STEINER	Forest Lawn, Glendale
Ford STERLING	Hollywood Memorial
Josef von STERNBERG	Westwood
McLean STEVENSON (*M.A.S.H.*)	Forest Lawn, Hollywood Hills
James STEWART	Forest Lawn, Glendale
Three STOOGES	Home of Peace; Hillside Memorial Park; Forest Lawn, Glendale
Dorothy STRATTEN	Westwood
Gloria STUART	Ashes returned to family
Mack SWAIN	Ashes scattered over the Pacific
Carl "Alfalfa" SWITZER	Hollywood Memorial
Constance TALMADGE	Hollywood Memorial
Natalie TALMADGE	Hollywood Memorial
Norma TALMADGE	Hollywood Memorial
William TALMAN	Forest Lawn, Hollywood Hills
Sharon TATE (Polanski)	Holy Cross
Art TATUM	Forest Lawn, Glendale

Elizabeth TAYLOR	Forest Lawn, Glendale
Robert TAYLOR	Forest Lawn, Glendale
William Desmond TAYLOR (Wm. Deane Tanner)	Hollywood Memorial
Irving THALBERG (and Norma Shearer)	Forest Lawn, Glendale
William "Buckwheat" THOMAS	Inglewood
Lawrence TIBBETT	Forest Lawn, Glendale
Dimitri TIOMKIN	Forest Lawn, Glendale
Mel TORME	Westwood
Ernest TORRENCE	Forest Lawn, Glendale
Spencer TRACY	Forest Lawn, Glendale
Henry TRAVERS	Forest Lawn, Glendale
Helen TRAVOLTA	Forest Lawn, Hollywood Hills
Claire TREVOR	Ashes scattered at sea
Forrest TUCKER	Forest Lawn, Hollywood Hills
Lana TURNER	Ashes returned to family
Ben TURPIN	Forest Lawn, Glendale
Ritchie VALENS	San Fernando Mission
Rudolph VALENTINO	Hollywood Memorial
Lee VAN CLEEF	Forest Lawn, Hollywood Hills
Vivian VANCE	Ashes scattered at sea
Yvette VICKERS (*Attack of the 50 Foot Woman*)	Ashes returned to family
Charles VIDOR	Home of Peace
Hervé de VILLECHAIZE	Body left to science and study of dwarfism; ashes to be scattered at sea
Paul WALKER	Forest Lawn, Hollywood Hills
Ray WALSTON (*My Favorite Martian*)	Ashes returned to family
Jack WARDEN	Ashes returned to family
Harry and Jack WARNER	Home of Peace
Harry S. WARREN	Westwood
John WAYNE	Pacific View, Newport Beach

Dennis WEAVER	Ashes returned to family
Clifton WEBB	Hollywood Memorial
Jack WEBB	Forest Lawn, Hollywood Hills
Mary WELLS	Forest Lawn, Glendale
James WHALE	Forest Lawn, Glendale
James WHITMORE	Ashes scattered at sea
Cornel WILDE	Westwood
Billy WILDER	Westwood
Esther WILLIAMS	Ashes scattered at sea
Chill WILLS	Grandview
Carl WILSON	Westwood
Dennis WILSON	Buried in the Pacific
Shelley WINTERS	Hillside
Robert WISE	Ashes returned to family
Anna May WONG	Rosedale
Ed WOOD	Ashes scattered
Edward D. WOOD	Ashes scattered at sea
Natalie WOOD (Wagner)	Westwood
Fay WRAY	Hollywood Memorial
William WYLER	Forest Lawn, Glendale
Ed and Keenan WYNN	Forest Lawn, Glendale
Loretta YOUNG	Holy Cross
Robert YOUNG	Forest Lawn, Glendale
Daryll F. ZANUCK (and Virginia Fox)	Westwood
Frank ZAPPA	Westwood

HOLLYWOOD MEMORIAL
PARK (HOLLYWOOD FOREVER)

Don ADAMS—Section 8, northeast of pond, by curb, angel statue, east of DeMille.

Rene ADOREE—Abbey of the Psalms, Sanctuary of Refuge, no. 219.

Agnes AYRES—Chapel Columbarium, lower south wall, niche 3, tier 3.

Mel BLANC—Pineland section (13), upright stone along Pineland Avenue.

Coral BROWNE—Ashes in Rose Garden, section 5, unmarked.

Louis CALHERN—Abbey of the Psalms, left side, urn, niche 308, tier 3, south wall.

Hannah CHAPLIN (mother of Charles)—Section 8, just north of Marion Davies.

Lana CLARKSON (died at Phil Spector's house)—Chapel Columbarium, second floor, south wall.

Iron Eyes CODY—Abbey of the Psalms, Sanctuary of Memories, corridor H-4-1, crypt 3301.

Harry COHN—Section 8, lot 86, south of lake, between Power and mausoleum.

Alan CROSLAND—section 13, grave 727S.

Viola DANA—Colonnade, north wall, niche 6, tier 4.

Bebe DANIELS—Chapel of the Psalms, Columbarium, 2nd floor, upper north wall, nos. 7 and 8, tier 3.

Joe DASSIN—Beth Olam, section 14, row 1, grave 79.

Marion DAVIES (Douras)—Section 8, east shore of lake, monument.

Cecil B. DEMILLE—Section 8, northwest shore of lake, monument.

Nelson EDDY—Section 8, southeast of lake, in front of bushes.

Douglas FAIRBANKS Sr. and Jr.—Section 11, Sunken Garden (west of Cathedral Mausoleum).

Peter FINCH—Cathedral Mausoleum, no. 1224, (opposite Valentino).

Victor FLEMING—Abbey of the Psalms, Sanctuary of Refuge, no. 2081.

Kathleen FREEMAN—Abbey of the Psalms, foyer, rotunda, tier G, niche 5.

Janet GAYNOR (Gregory)—Section 8, lot 193, near lake, black/white marker, a few rows forward of DeMille, under conifers, halfway between DeMille and Mansfield; to left is Adrian.

Lita GREY (Chaplin), and Charles CHAPLIN Jr.—Abbey of the Psalms, Corridor E-2 1065, Sanctuary of Trust, bottom tier (with mother).

Joan HACKETT—Abbey of the Psalms, Sanctuary of Faith, D3 2314.

Mildred HARRIS—Crypt in the Abbey of the Psalms, Refuge 740.

John HUSTON—Section 8, lot 6, sixteen rows to right of, and one down from, Adolphe Menjou, near big Kendall-Bell monument.

Don LAFONTAINE (voiceover for trailers)—Section 13, lot 747, space 12.

Barbara LA MARR—Cathedral Mausoleum, no. 1308, by window.

Jesse LASKY—Abbey of the Psalms, left side, Sanctuary of Light, 4386 E4.

Florence LAWRENCE (The Biograph Girl)—Section 2W, lot 300, east of entrance, along north wall, in line with Cohn.

Henry LEHRMAN—To immediate left of Virginia Rappe.

Elmo LINCOLN (the first Tarzan)—Colonnade, north wall, niche A.

Peter LORRE—Cathedral Mausoleum, Alcove of Remembrance, small plaque in bottom row.

Ben LYON—Chapel of the Psalms; with Bebe Daniels.

Jayne MANSFIELD—Pink marker by water, near DeMille, next to bush (marker only).

June MATHIS—Cathedral Mausoleum, no. 1199 (next to Valentino).

Hattie McDANIEL—Memorial by lake, opposite Fairbanks.

Darren McGAVIN—Just behind Maila Nurmi.

Adolphe MENJOU—Section 8, lot 11, northwest shore of lake, third row from curb, in line with bridge and Mattoon Bench, under tree.

Paul MUNI—Section 14, row OO, grave 57, in line with two eastern palm trees.

Maila NURMI (Vampira; Syrjaniemi)—Section 7, lot 203, space 1, by curb (just left of brown monument to Hovanesyan).

Eleanor POWELL—Cathedral Mausoleum, "Book Urn," left side of main hall, near last statue, niche 432, tier 3.

Tyrone POWER—Section 8, east shore of lake, bench monument.

Johnny RAMONE—Statue between lake and Fairbanks.

Virginia RAPPE—Section 8, lot 257, northeast shore of lake (first row), by Celtic cross.

Nelson RIDDLE—Section T1, niche 702, tier 7, Beth Olam Mausoleum (south entrance of Abbey of the Psalms; turn right; small alcove of cremations on left; right side of alcove, four feet up, near end of wall).

Harold ROSSON—Section 8, lot 44.

Ann SHERIDAN—Columbarium, upper east wall, tier 3, niche 24.

Benjamin "Bugsy" SIEGEL—Beth Olam Mausoleum, open book, M2-1087.

Ford STERLING—Ashes in the Chapel of the Psalms (unmarked, communal niche L, column 2, colonnade).

Carl "Alfalfa" SWITZER—Section 6, near southwest corner, along south edge, under little conifers.

Constance, Natalie and Norma TALMADGE—Abbey of the Psalms, Sanctuary of Eternal Love, G7 (family room).

William Desmond TAYLOR (William Deane Tanner)—Cathedral Mausoleum, second corridor on right, 594.

Rudolph VALENTINO—Cathedral Mausoleum, southeast corner, no. 1205.

Clifton WEBB—Abbey of the Psalms, left side, Sanctuary of Peace, G6 2350.

Daeida WILCOX (Beveridge)—Cathedral Mausoleum, crypt 989.

Harvey WILCOX—Cathedral Mausoleum, crypt 990.

Fay WRAY—Bench and willow tree by southwest corner of lake, near Ramone.

FOREST LAWN GLENDALE

Robert ALDA—Garden of Ascension, lot 9101, not far from Ted Knight.

Gracie ALLEN—With George Burns (Freedom Mausoleum, Sanctuary of Heritage, no. 20360-2).

Laverne and Maxine ANDREWS (The Andrews Sisters)—Great Mausoleum, Columbarium of Memory, niche 20390.

Minta Durfee ARBUCKLE—Ashes in Columbarium of Constancy, Great Mausoleum, niche 17743.

James ARNESS—Great Mausoleum, Jasmine Terrace, Sanctuary of Abiding Hope, crypt 16174.

Theda BARA (Brabin)—Great Mausoleum, Columbarium of Memory, near front.

Joseph BARBERA—Ashes in Great Mausoleum, Holly Terrace, Corridor of Glory, crypt 14451.

Binnie BARNES—With Mike Frankovich in the Joe E. Brown monument (elaborate white marker, Sunrise Slope, outside Great Mausoleum).

L. Frank BAUM (Author of *The Wizard of Oz*)—Section G-83, large granite marker.

Warner BAXTER—Garden of Memory, lawn crypt 579.

Wallace BEERY—Vale of Memory section, on periphery of Great Mausoleum, 2086-5.

Clara BLANDICK (Auntie Em)—Columbarium of Security, Great Mausoleum.

Joan BLONDELL—Cremation niche, Columbarium of Evening Star, Courts of Honor, above statue on left, top tier.

Eric BLORE—Cremation niche, Columbarium of Consecration, Great Mausoleum.

Betty BLYTHE—Cremation niche, Columbarium of Consecration, Great Mausoleum.

Humphrey BOGART—Urn in Garden of Memory (private), to left of statue of woman under a shell, Columbarium of Eternal Light, niche 647G.

Gutzon BORGLUM (creator and sculptor of Mt. Rushmore)—Under *Last Supper* window, Great Mausoleum.

Clara BOW—Freedom Mausoleum, Sanctuary of Heritage, no. 20353-2.

William BOYD (Hopalong Cassidy)—Sanctuary of Sacred Promise, large marble drawer to left, Great Mausoleum.

Rand BROOKS—Columbarium of Patriots, Court of Freedom.

Clarence BROWN—Base of classical marble statue, Columbarium of Evening Star, Gardens of Honor (unmarked).

Joe E. BROWN—Elaborate white marker, Sunrise Slope, outside Great Mausoleum (just south of Aimee Semple MacPherson).

George BURNS—Freedom Mausoleum, Sanctuary of Heritage, no. 20360-2.

Francis X. BUSHMAN—Freedom Mausoleum, basement, Sanctuary of Gratitude, right side, third row.

Jack CARSON—Great Mausoleum, Columbarium of Memory, near middle.

Lon CHANEY Sr.—Unmarked crypt no. 6407, Sanctuary of Meditation, Great Mausoleum.

Charley CHASE (Parrott)—Sunrise Slope, 72-5.

Nat King COLE—Freedom Mausoleum, Sanctuary of Heritage, no. 20369-2.

Russ COLUMBO—Great Mausoleum, Sanctuary of Vespers.

Sam COOKE—Garden of Memory, in lawn near wall, more or less opposite Sammy Davis Jr.

George CUKOR—Unmarked, crypt D, in Garden of Constancy, in the locked Garden of Honor, off Freedom Way.

Robert CUMMINGS—Ashes in Great Mausoleum, Columbarium of Sanctity, niche 21505.

Michael CURTIZ—Whispering Pines, 1178-8.

Dorothy DANDRIDGE—Cremation niche, Columbarium of Victory, Freedom Mausoleum, back wall, to right of statue, above Levi.

Jane DARWELL (Patti Woodard)—Whispering Pines, 1817-2, close to road.

Jim DAVIS (Jock Ewing)—Third floor, top of stairs, small vault, Iris Columbarium 24961, Great Mausoleum.

Sammy DAVIS Jr.—Statue, Gardens of Honor.

William DEMAREST—Sunrise Slope 3105.

Walt DISNEY—Just outside of, and left of entrance to, Freedom Hall Mausoleum.

DOLLY SISTERS—Great Mausoleum, Cathedral Corridor, statue on right.

Billy DOVE (Lillian Bohny Kenaston)—Freedom Mausoleum, lower level, Sanctuary of Freedom, crypt 21796, at bottom of stairs, just above eye level.

Marie DRESSLER—Great Mausoleum, Sanctuary of Benediction, right side.

W. C. FIELDS—Gold-covered niche in center of the Columbarium of Nativity (a little alcove down main, central hall, second floor, to left of Hall of Inspiration), Great Mausoleum.

Larry FINE (The 3 Stooges)—Freedom Mausoleum, basement, Sanctuary of Liberation, bottom, four rows in.

Errol FLYNN—Bronze statue, Court of Freedom, Garden of Everlasting Peace.

Rudolf FRIML—Under *Last Supper* window, Great Mausoleum.

Clark GABLE—Great Mausoleum, Sanctuary of Trust.

John GILBERT—Whispering Pines section, just below crest of hill, fifteen rows up from curb, north side, no. 1107 or 1102-4.

Hermione GINGOLD—Sanctuary of the Holy Spirit, second floor, Great Mausoleum.

Sam GOLDWYN—unmarked gated corner plot (crypt B) in Garden of Constancy, in the locked Garden of Honor, off Freedom Way.

Sid GRAUMAN—Great Mausoleum, Sanctuary of Benediction.

Sydney GREENSTREET—Utility niche, no markers (vaultage), Great Mausoleum storage area.

Jean HARLOW—Great Mausoleum, Sanctuary of Benediction.

Edith HEAD (Ihnen)—Cathedral Slope 1675-1.

Jean HERSHOLT—Monument across from the *Last Supper*, entrance to the Great Mausoleum.

Edward Everett HORTON—Whispering Pines section, 984-1 (not far from Mix and Oakie).

Michael JACKSON—Great Mausoleum, Holly Terrace (locked area).

Jennifer JONES—Ashes in Selznick family plot, Great Mausoleum, Sanctuary of Trust.

Gus KAHN—Whispering Pines, 757-5, near Nazimova.

Terry Allen KATH (Lead singer of *Chicago*)—Garden of Remembrance, Court of Christus, north side.

Ted KNIGHT (*Mary Tyler Moore Show*)—Garden of Ascension 9127, immediately to right of entrance.

Alan LADD—Freedom Mausoleum, Sanctuary of Heritage, no. 20358-2.

Louis L'AMOUR—By Memorial Terrace entrance of Great Mausoleum.

Carole LANDIS—Everlasting Love Section, 814-6, roadside.

Harold LLOYD—Begonia Corridor, 767-772, Great Mausoleum.

Carole LOMBARD—Next to Clark Gable (Great Mausoleum, Sanctuary of Trust).

Anita LOUISE (and Buddy ADLER)—Garden of Memory, statue in Little Garden of Tranquility, not far from McLaglen.

Ernst LUBITSCH—Eventide Section, 2896-2.

Ida LUPINO—Ashes scattered on her mother's grave, Constance Emerald Lupino, next to Errol Flynn, Garden of Everlasting Peace.

Jeanette MACDONALD—Freedom Mausoleum, Sanctuary of Heritage, no. 20364-2.

Mary MACLAREN—Dawn of Tomorrow section, crypt 7428.

Aimee Semple MACPHERSON—Sunrise Slope, in front of Great Mausoleum.

Quinn MARTIN—Great Mausoleum, Sanctuary of Refuge.

Chico MARX—Freedom Mausoleum, basement, Sanctuary of Worship, no. 22018.

Gummo MARX—Freedom Mausoleum, Basement, Sanctuary of Brotherhood, no. 21057 (across the corridor from Chico).

Mike MAZURKI—Columbarium of Victory, Freedom Mausoleum.

Victor MCLAGLEN—Columbarium of Eternal Light, Garden of Memory, niche 641 (next to Bogart).

Vincente MINNELLI—Garden of Enduring Faith, outer terraces of Triumphant Faith, to right of statue of man holding child.

Tom MIX—Whispering Pines section, middle of hilltop, southwest end.

Clayton MOORE (The Lone Ranger)—Garden of Everlasting Peace, west end of lawn, in center, in front of Morgenroth statue.

Alla NAZIMOVA—Whispering Pines, marker 1689.

Jack OAKIE (Lewis Delaney Offield)—Whispering Pines section, top of hill, near Tom Mix, 1066.

Merle OBERON (Wolders)—Gardens of Remembrance, almost opposite Kath, by south (outer) wall.

Lilli PALMER-Thompson—Commemoration, across Freedom Way from Tracy, opposite tree-trunk receptacle.

Alexander PANTAGES—Great Mausoleum, Sanctuary of Benediction.

Mary PICKFORD (Rogers)—"Motherhood" monument (three adults and four children) in locked Garden of Memory, to left of "Mystery of Life" statue.

Dick POWELL—Top tier, Columbarium of Honor, Courts of Honor (reads "God is Love"), back wall, top right.

Wallace REID—Black urn, Azalea Corridor, alcove B, Great Mausoleum.

Charles and Wesley RUGGLES—Garden of Memory, in ground, not far from Bogart.

S. Z. SAKALL (Waiter in *Casablanca*)—next to Ruggles (Garden of Memory, in ground).

David O. SELZNICK—Great Mausoleum, Sanctuary of Trust.

Norma SHEARER—With Irving Thalberg (Great Mausoleum, Sanctuary of Benediction).

Red SKELTON—Great Mausoleum, Sanctuary of Meditation (near Harlow and Thalberg).

Lionel STANDER—Court of Honor, lawn, 7246, by tree.

Jules STEIN—Garden of Memory, next to Pickford.

Max STEINER—Sanctuary of Enduring Faith, Great Mausoleum (near William Boyd).

James STEWART—Wee Kirk churchyard, plot 8, in front of the "archer" statue on the hilltop.

Art TATUM—Sanctuary of Peaceful Rest, Jasmine Terrace 16107A, Great Mausoleum.

Elizabeth TAYLOR—Great Mausoleum, angel statue "In Memoria" by entrance to *Last Supper* hall (unmarked).

Robert TAYLOR—Court of Freedom, Garden of Honor, Columbarium of the Evening Star, by Greek statue of woman under shell (private).

Irving THALBERG—Great Mausoleum, Sanctuary of Benediction.

Lawrence TIBBETT—Whispering Pines, downhill, marker 794.

Dimitri TIOMKIN—Columbarium of Memory, Great Mausoleum.

Ernest TORRENCE—Ashes in Columbarium of Prayer, bottom tier, Great Mausoleum.

Spencer TRACY—Court of Freedom, by gate), near Freedom Hall Mausoleum.

Henry TRAVERS (Angel from *It's a Wonderful Life*)—Columbarium of Nativity, across from W. C. Fields.

Ben TURPIN—Azelia Corridor, family room 9, Great Mausoleum.

Mary WELLS—Columbarium of Patriots, 35686, Freedom Mausoleum.

James WHALE—Cremation niche, Columbarium of Memory, Great Mausoleum.

William WYLER—Eventide Section, 2998-1.

Ed WYNN—Center niche on right wall, Columbarium of Dawn, second floor, Great Mausoleum.

Keenan WYNN—Above Ed Wynn (center niche on right wall, Columbarium of Dawn, second floor, Great Mausoleum).

Robert YOUNG—Graceland Section, lot 5905.

FOREST LAWN, HOLLYWOOD HILLS

Iris ADRIAN—Ashes in Columbarium of Radiant Dawn, 61905, Courts of Remembrance.

Leon AMES—Ashes in Columbarium of Valor, G64443, Courts of Remembrance.

Morey AMSTERDAM—Courts of Remembrance, crypt 3632, furthest northeast section, same court as Broccoli and Steiger.

Gene AUTRY—Sheltering Hills, lot 1048.

Frederick B. "Tex" AVERY—Gentleness Section, 863 (Evergreen Drive).

Lucille BALL (Morton)—Ashes were in Columbarium of Radiant Dawn, G62423, Courts of Remembrance, but now removed to New York State.

Noah BEERY Sr. (and Jr.; unmarked)—Sheltering Hills section, 930.

Ralph BELLAMY—Murmuring Trees Section, 8687.

Albert "Cubby" BROCCOLI—Family monument, easternmost court, Courts of Remembrance.

Godfrey CAMBRIDGE—Murmuring Trees Section, 5443, west of chapel, up the road, far behind and diagonally to right of Heidt memorial.

David CARRADINE—Lincoln Terrace, lot 5144, space 1.

Ray COLLINS (Lt. Tragg in *Perry Mason*)—Left of Stan Laurel, garden of Heritage 909–910, third level.

William CONRAD—Lincoln Terrace Section, on lawn, left of left path, by last tree before Lincoln.

Benjamin S. "Scatman" CROTHERS—Lincoln Terrace, halfway up on left of left path.

Bette DAVIS—Courts of Remembrance, left of entrance (large white sarcophagus with statue on it).

Brad DAVIS—Court of Remembrance, Columbarium of Valor, niche G64054.

Sandra DEE—Court of Remembrance, Sanctuary of Enduring Protection, wall crypt 3739.

Roy DISNEY—Sheltering Hills 125.

Michael Clarke DUNCAN—Courts of Remembrance, Sanctuary of Treasured Love, wall crypt 2949.

Dan DURYEA—Morning Light Section, 7383, eighteen rows up.

Richard FARNSWORTH—Columbarium of Purity, niche 63294 (three in from right edge, eight rows up).

Marty FELDMAN—Garden of Heritage 5400, road level, left of Washington Monument, in front of second garden, near wall, just left of first tree.

Reginald GARDINER—Sanctuary of Reflection, near Prinze/Raft. 3322.

Andy GIBB—Courts of Remembrance, external wall, facing west, 2534, second row from bottom.

T. Marvin HATLEY (composer of Laurel and Hardy theme song)— To right of Liberace (second court, Courts of Remembrance, big white sarcophagus and statue), vault 3405.

George F. "Gabby" HAYES—Hillside Section, plot 4972, eleven rows up.

Rex INGRAM—Court of Liberty, third level, to left of Stan Laurel, across path.

Bob KANE (creator of Batman)—Court of Liberty, lot 1310 (behind Stan Laurel), with Batman logo on marker.

Buster KEATON—Just to right of (and below) Washington Monument, first level, Court of Valor, no. 5512, row nearest the wall, between wall and road.

Ernie KOVACS—Down lawn across Vista Lane, facing Court of Remembrance, nearly across from water tower.

Dorothy LAMOUR (Howard)—Enduring Faith Section, 387.

Fritz LANG—Enduring Faith Section, 3818, up hill by road.

Walter LANTZ—Columbarium of Radiant Dawn, Courts of Remembrance.

Charles LAUGHTON—Court of Reverence, no. 3010 (Courts of Remembrance).

Stan LAUREL—Court of Liberty 912, near Hall of Liberty, to right of, and behind, Washington Monument.

Wladziu Valentino LIBERACE—Courts of Remembrance, second court, big white sarcophagus and statue.

Julie LONDON (and Bobby Troup)—Columbarium of Providence, to right of door as one exits.

Marjorie MAIN (Mary T. Krebs)—Enduring Faith Section, 2083/4.

Strother MARTIN—Columbarium of Radiant Dawn, G62420, Courts of Remembrance.

Brittany MURPHY—Bright Eternity, lot 7402, grave 1.

Ozzie and Harriet NELSON—Revelation Section, 3540, thirteen rows up from road.

Rick (Eric Hilliard) NELSON—Revelation Section, 3538, fifteen rows up from road.

Brock PETERS—Revelation Section, 3529.

Snub POLLARD—Sheltering Hills Section, 545.

Freddie PRINZE—Courts of Remembrance, Sanctuary of Light, no. 2355.

George RAFT—To immediate right of Freddie Prinze (Courts of Remembrance, Sanctuary of Light, no. 2355).

John RITTER—Court of Liberty, lot 1622 (to the right of Stan Laurel, through door, on other side of enclosure to left).

Joe E. ROSS (*Car 54*)—Summerland Section, 148/9.

Miklos ROZSA—Blessed Assurance 1656-1.

SABU (Dastigar)—Sheltering Hills Section, 482, under big tree.

George SAVALAS—Lincoln Terrace 4596.

Telly SAVALAS—Garden of Heritage 1281, second level (wall and lawn markers)

Rod STEIGER—Courts of Remembrance, Columbarium of Providence, niche G65094 (left of statue in right wall at eye level).

McLean STEVENSON (*M.A.S.H.*)—Columbarium of Valor niche, Courts of Remembrance.

William TALMAN (Hamilton Berger of *Perry Mason*)—Garden of Heritage, first level, near Washington Monument.

Helen TRAVOLTA—Up hill from Roy Disney (Sheltering Hills 125), to right of Smiley Burnette in 266.

Forrest TUCKER—Columbarium of Radiant Dawn, G62135 (near Pamela Britton), Courts of Remembrance.

Lee VAN CLEEF—Serenity section 156 (near entrance of Courts of Remembrance).

Paul WALKER—Court of Liberty, Gardens of Heritage, Lot 393.

Jack WEBB—Sheltering Hills, plot 1999.

WESTWOOD

Eddie ALBERT—In lawn, just north of Sammy Cahn (section D, lot 81, four graves west of Donna Reed).

Eve ARDEN (West)—Ashes buried with husband Brooks West, section D, lot 81 (unmarked).

Lew AYRES—In lawn, halfway between the Cantor Mausoleum (by entrance) and the office.

Jim BACKUS—Section D, lot 203, southwest corner, just north of the urn garden.

Richard BASEHART—Urn garden, left middle.

John BOLES—Sanctuary of Serenity, crypt C-62.

Ray BRADBURY—In garden, east of Peggy Lee.

Fannie BRICE—Garden of Serenity.

Les BROWN (bandleader)—Plaque east of Brian Keith.

Sebastian CABOT—Urn garden, top row, lot 200, grave 6, opposite Armand Hammer monument.

Sammy CAHN—Section D, lot 81, four graves west of Donna Reed.

Truman CAPOTE—Outer west wall of mausoleum, to left of O'Rourke.

John CASSAVETES—Lot 308, just right of Eva Gabor.

James COBURN—Bench opposite Peggy Lee's.

Ray CONNIFF—South edge of lawn, opposite O'Connor.

Richard CONTE—Section D, lot 62, grave 2, just east of Natalie Wood.

Bob CRANE (*Hogan's Heroes*)—Lawn, just southeast of Natalie Wood, three graves west of Richard Conte, between Misner and Dye Sr.

Norma CRANE—Lawn, immediately east of Natalie Wood, near tree.

Rodney DANGERFIELD—To right of Farrah Fawcett.

Dominique DUNNE—Section D, lot 189, near bottom of lawn, in line with Natalie Wood, between Stratten and chapel.

Peter FALK—Just to left of Billy Wilder.

Farrah FAWCETT—By roadside, east of chapel, to right of Merv Griffin.

Jay C. FLIPPEN—Same wall as Marilyn Monroe (section A, Corridor of Memories, crypt 24).

Eva GABOR—Just in front of, and to right of, Hammer Mausoleum.

Paul GLEASON ("Clarence Beeks")—In lawn, immediately west of Carl Wilson (in line with Marilyn Monroe, and just left of Minnie Riperton).

Merv GRIFFIN—By roadside, left of Farrah Fawcett, east of chapel.

Percy HELTON—Sanctuary of Remembrance.

Nunnally JOHNSON—Sanctuary of Tranquility.

Louis JOURDAN Jr.—In lawn, in line with and to south of Richard Conte (section D, lot 62, grave 2).

Brian KEITH—In new garden, small plaque in inner north wall above one for daughter Daisy.

Stan KENTON—Ashes in rose garden, with commemorative tablet under bush.

Don KNOTTS—In lawn, near curb, left of Hammer Mausoleum.

Burt LANCASTER—Ashes in lawn, just opposite Sanctuary of Love, northeast of Minnie Riperton.

Peter LAWFORD—Was in outer west wall of mausoleum section; ashes now scattered over the Pacific.

Irving "Swifty" LAZAR—Ground plaque near lot 236, between Hammer and Capote.

Peggy LEE—Ashes marked by a bench in new garden.

Jack LEMMON—Close to chapel.

Oscar LEVANT—Sanctuary of Love, bottom right, crypt 26-A.

Karl MALDEN—Garden of Serenity (just round corner from George C. Scott, on right, in line with chapel).

Janet MARGOLIN—Section D, urn garden, just right of Burt Lancaster.

Dean MARTIN—Sanctuary of Love, near his parents (Crocetti, in Sanctuary of Peace).

Walter MATTHAU—Garden of Serenity, frontage, near Hyman.

Terry MCQUEEN—Just to right of Natalie Wood (section D, lot 60, north edge of lawn, under large tree), buried with a vial of her father Steve McQueen's ashes.

Allan MELVIN (*Bilko*)—Lawn, in line with Sanctuary of Devotion, immediately northwest of Lloyd Nolan.

Lewis MILESTONE—Sanctuary of Tranquility.

Marilyn MONROE—Section A, Corridor of Memories, crypt 24.

Jeff MORRIS—South end of lawn, by road, in line with Marilyn Monroe.

Lloyd NOLAN—Section D, lot 84, lawn, just southeast of Natalie Wood and Richard Conte.

Carroll O'CONNOR (Archie Bunker)—Between Wilder and Lemmon, near chapel.

Roy ORBISON—Section D, lot 97 (unmarked, twenty-five feet east of Frank Zappa, above Frank Wright Tuttle), in line with tree.

Heather O'ROURKE (*Poltergeist*)—Outer west wall of mausoleum section.

Donna REED (Asmus)—Section D, lot 142, lawn, in line with Lloyd Nolan, southwest of Natalie Wood.

Buddy RICH—Sanctuary of Tranquility, bottom right, second from end.

Minnie RIPERTON—Section D, lot 173, southeast corner of lawn, in line with Marilyn Monroe.

George C. SCOTT—In frontage of the new gardens, third grave from east, next to Hyman (unmarked).

Robert STACK—In eye-level book in top-left glass case facing door, Room of Prayer.

Josef von STERNBERG—Sanctuary of Remembrance.

Dorothy STRATTEN—Section D, lot 170, on central lawn, west of Minnie Riperton, in line with Sanctuary of Devotion.

Mel TORME—On the lawn close to Truman Capote.

Harry S. WARREN—First Sanctuary (Tenderness), right side, bottom row.

Cornel WILDE—Plaque in urn garden, in line with Eva Gabor.

Billy WILDER—Ashes buried near chapel, next to O'Connor and Lemmon.

Carl WILSON (The Beach Boys)—Lawn, in line with Marilyn Monroe and just left of Minnie Riperton.

Natalie WOOD (Wagner)—Section D, lot 60, north edge of lawn, under large tree.

Darryl ZANUCK (and Virginia Fox)—Section D, lot 41, just west of Natalie Wood.

Frank ZAPPA—Section D, lot 100, near Backus, and near big tree, halfway between office and entrance, just above Charles Bassler and next to Lew Ayres (unmarked).

HILLSIDE

Gene BARRY—Canaan Garden Mausoleum, crypt H390A.

Jack BENNY (and wife Mary)—Main Mausoleum, end of Hall of Graciousness, first floor.

Milton BERLE—Ashes in crypt in Acacia Gardens, just behind and to right of huge marriage mural, MM 354B, three levels up, eye level.

Ben BLUE—Main Mausoleum, Columbarium of Graciousness 810.

Eddie CANTOR—Main Mausoleum, Graciousness 207, to left of Jack Benny, opposite stairs.

Jeff CHANDLER (Ira Grossel)—Main Mausoleum, Graciousness, second floor, 4015.

Cyd CHARISSE—Court of Matriarchs, S401-B, ground floor, first alcove on right, fourth row up, next to wall.

Max FACTOR—Courts of the Book, Isaiah-U-314, crypt.

Percy FAITH—Outside, on the hill, in small garden, Honor 407.

Arthur FREED—Same row as Percy Faith, Honor 418.

(Isadore) Friz FRELENG—Canaan E 249 (back of cemetery).

Jerry GOLDSMITH—Garden of Memories, Court of Truth, second floor, wall FF, crypt 265.

Lorne GREENE—Courts of the Book, 5-800-8B (in lawn).

Moe HOWARD (3 Stooges)—Alcove of Love, C-233.

David JANSSEN—Left side of open-air part of mausoleum, opposite entrance, Memorial Court 516, bottom tier.

George JESSEL—Three drawers above David Janssen.

Al JOLSON—Waterfall Monument.

Michael LANDON—Private room with glass door inside mausoleum complex, off Courts of the Book.

Jerry LEIBER—Garden of Solomon, block 9, plot 5, space 1.

Vic MORROW—Mount Olive Section, block 5-80-1.

Suzanne PLESHETTE—Abraham 127B (just above Jolson, to right of mausoleum entrance).

Dick SHAWN—Same wall as Janssen, Memorial Court 734 (to the right, top tier).

Allan SHERMAN—Mausoleum, niche 513: enter mausoleum rotunda, turn right into Sanctuary of Benevolence then left into Corridor of Contentment, walk down three sections to Columbarium of Hope on left: five rows from bottom, thirteen rows from left, a tiny plaque.

Robert SHERMAN—Canaan, H303, three rows up, at right-corner end of wall.

Dinah SHORE—Crypt, Courts of the Book, Isaiah V-247.

Aaron SPELLING—Mausoleum, Hall of Reverence, FF J1.

Shelley WINTERS—Hillside slope, block 11, plot 358, grave 8 (in line with bench to left of door as you face building, eighth row from top).

HOLY CROSS

Richard ARLEN—Section T, tier 57, grave 130.

Mary ASTOR—Section N-523-5 (in line with corner of mausoleum).

Ray BOLGER—Mausoleum, left side of chapel, section 35, bottom row (F2Z).

Charles BOYER—St. Anne's Garden, tier 186, grave 5 (near wall).

Scott BRADY—Mausoleum, block 156, crypt B-7.

Keefe BRASSELLE (John D. Brasselli)—Section R, tier 29, grave 168.

John CANDY—Mausoleum (same room as MacMurray), crypt D5.

MacDonald CAREY—Grotto side, 19-196 (to right of and behind Rita Hayworth).

Marguerite CHAPMAN—Mausoleum, block 28, crypt 83.

Jackie COOGAN (John Leslie)—Section F, tier 56, grave 47 (behind the *Pieta*).

Harry L. "Bing" CROSBY (and Dixie Lee Crosby)—Grotto, lot 119, grave 1.

Joan DAVIS (Williams)—Mausoleum, block 46, crypt D-1 (to left of Mario Lanza).

Jimmy DURANTE—Section F (St. Joseph), tier 96, grave 6 (near road).

Richard EGAN—Section M, tier 37, grave 139.

Joe FLYNN—Section B, lot 320, grave 10.

John FORD—Section M, lot 304, grave 5.

Jack HALEY—Grotto, lot 100, grave 2.

June HAVER (MacMurray)—Mausoleum, room 7, crypt D1.

Rita HAYWORTH—To immediate right of the grotto, in front of angel.

Jose ITURBI—Mausoleum, block 16, crypt E-1.

Lindley "Spike" JONES—Mausoleum, block 70, crypt A-4, near top.

Edgar KENNEDY—Section D, lot 193, grave 7 (under tree).

Mario LANZA—Mausoleum, block 46, crypt D-2 (right side of altar).

Jim and Marian JORDAN—St. Anne's Garden, tier 153, grave 2.

Gene LOCKHART—Section D, lot 280, grave 12.

Frank LOVEJOY—Section P, lot 306, grave 5.

Bela LUGOSI—Grotto, tier 120, grave 1.

William LUNDIGAN—Section D, lot 269, grave 3.

Fred MacMURRAY—Mausoleum, block 84, room 7L, crypt D2.

Al MARTINO—Mausoleum of Our Divine Savior, ground floor, block 13, crypt D-15 (fourth row up, far right).

Leo McCAREY—Section T, T134-44.

Ann MILLER—Section F, T57, grave 58 (next to mother and miscarried baby of 1946).

Ricardo MONTALBAN—Section EE (just north of and across road from top left part of CC 2) tier 3, grave 21.

Edmond O'BRIEN—Section F, tier 54, grave 50 (behind the Pieta).

Pat O'BRIEN—Section F, tier 56, grave 62 (behind the Pieta).

Barney E. OLDFIELD—Section D, lot 290, grave 11 (under tree).

Edward "KID" ORY—Grotto, lot 59, grave 4.

Hermes PAN—Mausoleum, block 127 D5, upstairs, to left of big altar frieze.

Louella PARSONS (Martin)—Section D, lot 235, grave 8.

Chris PENN—Section CC, tier 54.

ZaSu PITTS (Woodall)—Grotto, lot 195, grave 1, by the wall, near Charles Boyer.

Rosalind RUSSELL (Brisson)—Section M, lot 536, grave 2 (at foot of crucifixion).

Gia SCALA—Section M, to right of cross, down a row, four markers to right of 580.

Mack SENNETT—Section N, lot 490, grave 1.

Sharon TATE (Polanski)—St. Anne's Garden, tier 152, grave 6.

Lawrence WELK—Center of section Y, 110-T9-Y, near flower shop.

Loretta YOUNG—Ashes buried unmarked in her mother's grave (Gladys Belzen, section F, tier 65, grave 49).

HOME OF PEACE (4334 WHITTIER BOULEVARD, LOS ANGELES)

Fanny BRICE—Was in niche no. 1109, between Corridor of Benevolence and Corridor of Harmony, in mausoleum; now in Westwood.

Jerome "CURLY" HOWARD (3 Stooges)—Right rear of cemetery (southwest corner, behind and to right of mausoleum), Western Jewish Institute, plot 1, five rows back.

Shemp HOWARD (3 Stooges)—Corridor of Eternal Life, Mausoleum. EW 215.

Carl LAEMMLE—Corridor of Love, mausoleum, family room at very end on right side.

Louis B. MAYER—Mausoleum, Corridor of Immortality, drawer SW 405, above eye level on the left.

Charles VIDOR and Harry WARNER—Small mausoleum, fifty yards from Jack Warner, section D, plot 16.

Jack WARNER—Black marble slab and memorial fountain, section C.

CALVARY (4201 WHITTIER BOULEVARD, LOS ANGELES)

Ethel BARRYMORE (Colt)—Main mausoleum, chapel, second floor, block 60, bottom row (3F).

John BARRYMORE—Marker in main mausoleum, second floor, first chapel to right of altar, near stairs, block 352, F-3; later, ashes buried, unmarked, in plot of parents and grandparents (Drew-Blythe) in Mt. Vernon Cemetery, Philadelphia.

Lionel BARRYMORE—Above John Barrymore's marker in main mausoleum.

Lou COSTELLO (Louis Francis Cristillo)—Main mausoleum, second floor, middle chapel to right of altar, high on left wall, block 354, crypt B-1.

Irene DUNNE—With husband Dr. Francis Griffin, mausoleum, near Christ Crucified window, second floor, on left.

Stepin FETCHIT (Lincoln Perry)—Section K, tier 13, grave 116 (unmarked).

John HODIAK—Main mausoleum, main hallway, block 352, D7.

Ferdinand "Jelly Roll" MORTON—Section N, lot 347-4: pass main mausoleum on right, look for 343 on curb at right, stop there and walk nine rows up to base of tree.

Mabel NORMAND (Cody)—Crypt in main mausoleum, main hallway, block 303 D7 second floor and sharp left.

Pola NEGRI (Mdivani)—Mausoleum, block 56, crypt E-19, second floor, St. Paul, beyond altar.

Ramon NOVARRO—Centre of section C, plot 586-5, just north of Hickson Arch, in line west of Pinkerton stone.

Mary PHILBIN—Mausoleum, block 35, crypt D-4.

SAN FERNANDO MISSION
(11160 STRANWOOD AVENUE, MISSION HILLS)

Ed BEGLEY—Section C, lot 402, fourteenth row from curb at no. 395.

William BENDIX—Section D, lot 247, grave 10 (near tree, fourteenth row from curb at 241).

Walter BRENNAN—Section D, lot 445, grave 8 (second row from curb).

Jerry COLONNA—Section B, lot 848, grave 7, fourteenth row in, halfway between 829 and 842 on curb.

Chuck CONNORS—Section J, T-20, grave 123

Carmine COPPOLA—Mausoleum block 28, crypt E4.

William FRAWLEY (*I Love Lucy*)—Section C, lot 66, grave 4 (six graves up from curb at 64).

Anita GARVIN (Stanley)—Section EE, row 67, grave 8.

Bob HOPE—Bob Hope Memorial Gardens.

Clarence "Ducky" NASH—Section 25, lot 47, grave F

Ritchie VALENS—Section C, across and down road from office and flower shop (plot 247, along curb and three rows in).

EDEN (11500 SEPULVEDA
BOULEVARD, MISSION HILLS)

Lenny "BRUCE" (Schneider)—Mount Nebo 298-C.

Harvey LEMBECK (Cpl. Barbella in "Bilko")—Mount Jerusalem, lot 419.

Groucho MARX—Columbarium, plaque at eye level, left side.

VALHALLA (10621 VICTORY BOULEVARD, NORTH HOLLYWOOD)

Bea BENADARET ("Betty Rubble")—Mausoleum of Hope, Garden of Love, row C, crypt 34.

Mae CLARKE—C-23-4-1.

CRISWELL (Chas. C. King)—Mausoleum, Niches of Remembrance, F-10, space 2.

Yakima CANUTT—Ashes in rose garden, wall plaque in columbarium.

Joe DeRITA (3 Stooges)—Garden of Rest, block D, section 338, lot 19.

Cliff EDWARDS (Jiminy Cricket)—Section D, near Heritage Fountain, eight rows in from curb marker 6411.

Oliver HARDY—Garden of Hope, lot 48, row D, plaque in ground and memorial slab in wall, immediately to right of path, near fountain.

Mae MURRAY—Block G, lot 6, section 6328.

MOUNT SINAI (5950 FOREST LAWN DRIVE, BURBANK)

Irwin ALLEN—Garden of Heritage, crypt, second level.

Lee J. COBB—Garden of Shemot, lot 421, by tree.

Mama Cass ELLIOT (Ellen Naomi Cohen)—Courts of TaNach area no. 7, edge of lawn, rear left corner, back row, second in from left.

Fritz FELD—Moses 16, lot 6520, space 2.

Phil SILVERS—Garden of Traditions, lot 1004, lawn crypt 1A.

CHAPEL OF THE PINES CREMATORY (1605 SOUTH CATALINA, LOS ANGELES)

Lionel ATWILL—Vaultage area (closed to public).

Nigel BRUCE—Vault no. 35167, Deodora Hall North, third row up.

Mae BUSCH (Tate)—Niche, Deodora Hall South, section R, no. 86.

Tom CONWAY—Vaultage area.

Margaret DUMONT—Vaultage area (closed to public).

James FINLAYSON—Vaultage area (unmarked).

Edmund GWENN (Santa Claus in *Miracle on 34th Street*)—Vaultage area.

Thomas MITCHELL—Vaultage area.

FOREST LAWN MEMORIAL PARK, CYPRESS (4471 LINCOLN AVENUE, CYPRESS)

Eddie COCHRAN—Tender Promise section, fourth row from wall, opposite Ascension Mosaic, large gravestone, Bl. 2996-4.

GRANDVIEW CEMETERY, GLENDALE (1341 GLENWOOD ROAD)

Leo G. CARROLL—Crypt A, section 15, under chapel in West Mausoleum (community niche, no marker).

Harry LANGDON—Ashes in niche 81, unit E, chapel section, West Mausoleum, just inside main door, dark wall of glass cases on left, bottom row, right of center.

Edna PURVIANCE (Squire)—Ashes in niche in chapel section, West Mausoleum, just inside main door, immediately left, third row in, sixth from top.

Chill WILLS—Buried outside, plot 27, row C, Garden of Devotion, in front of North Mausoleum, right front garden of small plaques, second in, northeast corner.

INGLEWOOD MEMORIAL PARK (720 E. FLORENCE AVENUE, INGLEWOOD)

Edgar BERGEN (Bergren)—131 Miramar Plot, grave no. 2, near List (which is near road).

Paul BERN—Mausoleum of the Golden West, east side, on very top of first glassed-in niches, F96, niche D.

Norman Spencer CHAPLIN (The Little Mouse)—Children's section, near office, Del Ivy lot 496.

Ray CHARLES—32A in Eternal Love, north 2E corner of Mausoleum of the Golden West.

Ella FITZGERALD—Sanctuary of the Bells, 1063 tier 2, Sunset Mission Mausoleum, level 2.

Hoot GIBSON—92 Magnolia Plot, grave no. 6.

Betty GRABLE—Mausoleum of the Golden West, east end, Sanctuary of Dawn, A-78.

Lucille LAVERNE (Queen in *Snow White*)—Center grave, division D, lot 2236, Palm Plot.

Gypsy Rose LEE—1087 Pinecrest Plot, grave no. 8.

Billy PRESTON—Garden of Peace, south end, row 151, tier 2.

Sugar Ray ROBINSON—Pinecrest, near middle.

Cesar ROMERO—Crematorium niche, Alcove of Music, Mausoleum of the Golden West, at east end, between the sanctuaries of Devotion and Reverence, in Alcove of Dreams.

William "Buckwheat" THOMAS—777 Acacia Slope, grave D, near far right corner, two rows from end, two rows in.

PACIFIC VIEW MEMORIAL PARK
(3500 PACIFIC VIEW DRIVE, NEWPORT BEACH)

John WAYNE—On lawn below Mausoleum of the Pacific, beside Charles Iverson IV, grave C, lot 573, Bayview Terrace.

ROSEDALE CEMETERY (1831 WEST WASHINGTON BOULEVARD, LOS ANGELES)

Eric CAMPBELL—Ashes in unidentified space.

Hattie McDANIEL—Section D, lot 23, near entrance, five rows in from curb, just across from office.

Andy RAZAF—Right of chapel, facing it, second row from wall, section V, lot 109.

Everett SLOANE—Cremation niche in the mausoleum, F NW-122.

Art TATUM—Marker in section 5, lot 173, twenty-eight spaces in on row 178; now in Forest Lawn, Glendale.

Anna May WONG—Near Tatum section 5, lot 136, grave 3NE (pink marble, Chinese inscription).

OAKWOOD MEMORIAL CEMETERY, CHATSWORTH (ANDORA AVENUE AT LASSEN)

Fred ASTAIRE (and Adele)—G-77.

Stephen BOYD—Cremation niche in columbarium, top left corner.

Ginger ROGERS—Section E, lot 303.

WOODLAWN MEMORIAL PARK, SANTA MONICA

Henry DANIELL—Ashes in section B, crypt 32, mausoleum (no marker, just a sealed crypt full of urns).

Glenn FORD—Mausoleum, basement, Twilight Crypt G-216, on right, second row from right, third row up.

William HAINES—Cremation niche in mausoleum, Columbarium Heavenly Gate, crypt 253, ground floor.

Paul HENREID—Section C-3M, lot 12, grave A.

Harvey KORMAN—Mausoleum second floor, grave 129, D-2 Unity, block 7: from elevator turn left, away from office, then turn right at Cherish; he is bottom row on the right, second from the window.

Doug McCLURE—Section 3-M, near Henreid.

MELROSE ABBEY, ANAHEIM

Carolyn JONES—Crypt in mausoleum, north patio 46 gg, bottom row.

ST. MATTHEW'S EPISCOPAL CHURCH, PACIFIC PALISADES (LOS ANGELES COUNTY)

Charlton HESTON—Ashes in urn garden, small plaque on corner of wall in columbarium.

WESTLAKE CEMETERY (5600 LINDERO CANYON ROAD, WESTLAKE VILLAGE)

Karen CARPENTER—Family mausoleum (drive across to far end, then left to waterfall).

Virginia MAYO—Garden of Gethsemane, plot 313, up main slope in front of office, in line with statue of Christ.

Harry NILSSON—Garden of Gethsemane, plot 830, grave, just over brow of hill and to right.

ETERNAL VALLEY MEMORIAL PARK (23287 SIERRA HIGHWAY, NEWHALL)

Tor JOHNSON—Whispering Pines, 177 (near top of slope).

Gene VINCENT—Garden of Repose, grave A91 (in line with old hearse).

RIVERSIDE NATIONAL CEMETERY (22495 VAN BUREN BOULEVARD, RIVERSIDE)

Woody STRODE—Section 46, row O, grave 283.

SUNSET HILLS MEMORIAL PARK, APPLE VALLEY

Roy ROGERS and Dale EVANS—Just inside entrance, to left, under trees.

OUT-OF-TOWNERS LIST

Judith ANDERSON	Ashes returned to Australia
Harry ANDREWS	St. Mary's Church, Salehurst, East Sussex, UK
Anna Maria Pier ANGELI	Cimetière des Bulvis, Rueil-Malmaison, France
Evelyn ANKERS	New section, grave 113, Makawao Veterans Cemetery, Makawao, Hawaii
Michelangelo ANTONIONI	Cimitero della Certosa, Ferrara, Friuli-Venezia Giulia, Italy
Roscoe "Fatty" ARBUCKLE	Ashes scattered at sea off Catalina, California
Louis ARMSTRONG	Flushing Cemetery, Queens, New York
Desi ARNAZ	Ashes scattered at sea off Baja California, Mexico
Peggy ASHCROFT	Ashes returned to family
Mischa AUER	Prospect Hill Cemetery, Gloversville, New York
Josephine BAKER	Monaco cemetery
Stanley BAKER	Cremated at Putney Vale, London
George BALANCHINE	Oakland Cemetery, near Sag Harbor, New York
Lucille BALL	Lakeview Cemetery, Highland Section, Jamestown, New York
Martin BALSAM	Niche 1360, Sanctuary of Abraham and Sarah (mausoleum), Forest Avenue, Paramus, New Jersey
Anne BANCROFT	Section 180, lot 6, Kensico Cemetery, Valhalla, New York
Tallulah BANKHEAD	St. Paul's Churchyard, Chestertown, Maryland
Leslie BANKS	Ashes buried in Worth-Matravers Graveyard, Swanage, Dorset, UK

Lex BARKER	Ashes returned to family
Ronnie BARKER	Ashes buried in urn in garden of Banbury Crematorium, Oxfordshire, UK
Peter BARKWORTH	Golders Green Crematorium, London
Jean-Louis BARRAULT (and Madeleine RENAUD)	Passy Cemetery, Paris.
John BARRYMORE	Ashes buried, unmarked, in Drew/ Blythe plot, Mt. Vernon Cemetery, Philadelphia
Freddie BARTHOLOMEW	Ashes buried in memorial garden of the United Congregational Church of Christ, Bradenton, Florida
James BASKETT (Uncle Remus)	Crown Hill Cemetery, Indianapolis, Indiana
Lina BASQUETTE	Ashes returned to family
Ralph BATES	Chiswick New Cemetery, Staveley Road, London
Anne BAXTER	Unity Chapel, Spring Green, Wisconsin
James BECK	Cremated at Putney Vale, London
Richard BECKINSALE	Plaque at Mortlake Crematorium, London
Barbara BEL GEDDES	Ashes scattered at New York farm
John BELUSHI	Abel's Hill Cemetery, Chilmark, Massachusetts
Constance BENNETT	Arlington National Cemetery, Arlington, Virginia
Jill BENNETT	Ashes scattered over River Thames, London
Joan BENNETT	Ashes returned to family
Brook BENTON	Ephesus A.M.E. Church, Lugoss, South Carolina

Ingmar BERGMAN	Farö Churchyard, Farö, Gotlands Lan, Sweden
Ingrid BERGMAN	Ashes scattered at sea off Danholmen, Sweden
Busby BERKELEY	Desert Memorial Park, Palm Springs (section A-14, lot no. 74)
Irving BERLIN	Woodlawn Cemetery, Bronx, New York (flat slab, Columbine Section, along Heather Avenue)
Leonard BERNSTEIN	Highest point of Greenwood cemetery, Brooklyn, New York
Claude BERRI	Cimetière de Bagneux, France
Billy BEVAN (Harris)	Oak Hill Cemetery, Escondido, California
Bill BIXBY	Ashes scattered at estate, Hana, Hawaii
Karen BLACK	Eternal Hills Memorial Park, Oceanside, San Diego County
Otis BLACKWELL	Woodlawn Cemetery, Nashville, Tennessee (crypt, third floor of mausoleum)
Dan BLOCKER	Woodman Cemetery, DeKalb, Texas
Dirk BOGARDE	Ashes scattered at his former farmhouse in Provence, France
Derek BOND	Putney Vale Cemetery and Crematorium, Wimbledon, London
Ward BOND (Edwin Ewart)	Ashes scattered over the Pacific.
Sonny BONO	Desert Memorial Park, Cathedral City, Palm Springs, California (near back, by enclosed waterfall, near palm tree, immediately right of fountain enclosure, B-35, lot 294)
Richard BOONE	Ashes scattered
BOURVIL (André Raimbourg)	Montainville, Yvelines, France

Wilfred BRAMBELL	East Finchley Cemetery, London, by tree
Neville BRAND	East Lawn Memorial Park, Sacramento, California
Marlon BRANDO	Ashes scattered in Death Valley and Tahiti
Rossano BRAZZI	Cimitero Prima Porta, Rome
Bernard BRESLAW	Golders Green Crematorium, London (east-central bed, section K, plot E46591)
Jean-Claude BRIALY	Montmartre Cemetery, Paris
Charles BRONSON	Brownsville Cemetery, West Windsor, Vermont
Louise BROOKS	Holy Sepulchre Cemetery, Rochester, New York
Virginia BRUCE	Ashes returned to family
Yul BRYNNER	Ashes buried under only tombstone in cemetery of medieval monastery of Saint-Michel-de-Bois-Aubry, Luzé, Indre-et-Loire, France
Horst BUCHHOLZ	Friedhof Heerstrasse, Trakehner Allee 1, Berlin
Luis BUÑUEL	Mexico City
Billie BURKE (and Florenz ZIEGFELD)	Kensico Cemetery, Lakeview Avenue, Valhalla, New York (under willow, end of Powhatan Avenue)
Raymond BURR	Ashes at Frasier Cemetery, New Westminster, British Columbia
Richard BURTON	Old cemetery, Céligny, Lac Leman, Switzerland
Peter BUTTERWORTH	Danehill Cemetery, East Sussex, UK
Spring BYINGTON	Body left to University of California, Irvine.
Bruce CABOT	Carlsbad Municipal Cemetery, Carlsbad, New Mexico

James CAGNEY	St. Francis of Assisi Mausoleum, Gate of Heaven Cemetery, Hawthorne, New York (exterior couch crypt in open alcove on right as you walk toward the mausoleum entrance near the front of the cemetery)
Cab CALLOWAY	Ashes returned to family
Frank CAPRA	Coachella Valley Cemetery, Coachella, California
Ahna CAPRI	Ashes returned to family
Hoagy CARMICHAEL	Rose Hill Cemetery, Bloomington, Indiana
Art CARNEY	Riverside Cemetery, Old Saybrook, Connecticut
Karen CARPENTER	Valley Oaks Memorial Park, Westlake Village, California
Madeline CARROLL	Cementeri de Calonge, Catalonia, Spain
Enrico CARUSO	Del Planto Cemetery, Naples
Jean-Pierre CASSEL	Roman Catholic Cemetery de Thoiry, Yvelines, Ile de France
John CAZALE	Holy Cross Cemetery, Malden, Massachusetts
Claude CHABROL	Père Lachaise Cemetery, Paris (10th section, near Chopin)
Charles CHAPLIN	Cemetery, Corsier-sur-Vevey, Lac Leman, Switzerland
Sydney CHAPLIN	Ashes buried in Montreux, Switzerland
Graham CHAPMAN	Ashes scattered over Mt. Snowdon (Wales) in a fireworks display.
Paddy CHAYEFSKY	Kensico Cemetery, Valhalla, New York
Virginia CHERRILL (Martini)	Ashes in Chapel mausoleum, Santa Barbara Cemetery (right wall, last before arch)

Maurice CHEVALIER	Marne La Coquette, France
Diane CILENTO	Highgate Cemetery East, London
Montgomery CLIFT	Friends Cemetery, Prospect Park, Brooklyn, New York
Rosemary CLOONEY	St. Patrick's Cemetery, Maysville, Kentucky
Nicholas COLASANTO (*Cheers*)	St. Anne's Cemetery, Cranston, Rhode Island
Claudette COLBERT	Buried with husband Joel Pressman in St. Peter's Parish churchyard, near Bridgetown, Barbados
Constance COLLIER	Islington Cemetery, London
Ronald COLMAN	Santa Barbara Cemetery, California (ridge section, oval lot 663).
Peter COOK	St. John-at-Hampstead Parish churchyard, London
Gary COOPER	Sacred Heart Cemetery, Southampton, Long Island, New York
Gladys COOPER	Hampstead Cemetery, London
Jackie COOPER	Arlington National Cemetery, Arlington, Virginia
Harry H. CORBETT	Penhurst Parish churchyard, East Sussex, UK
Joseph COTTEN	Ashes to Blanford Cemetery, Petersburg, Virginia
Hazel COURT	Ashes scattered at sea
Wally COX	Ashes kept by Marlon Brando in Tahiti
Broderick CRAWFORD	Ferndale Cemetery, Johnstown, New York
Joan CRAWFORD	Ferncliff Cemetery, Hartsdale, New York (old wing, main mausoleum, ground floor, unit 8, alcove E)
Laura Hope CREWS (Aunt Pittypat)	Cypress Lawn, Colma, California

Jim CROCE	Philadelphia Memorial Park, Frazer, Pennsylvania
Robert CULP	Sunset View Cemetery, El Cerrito, Contra Costa City, California
Tony CURTIS	Palm Memorial Park (Green Valley), Las Vegas (legacy area, space PG 10, row 3)
Peter CUSHING	Ashes at Seasalter Old Church, Whitstable, Kent, UK
Gerard DAMIANO	Fort Myers Memorial Gardens, Fort Myers, Florida
Linda DARNELL	Union Hill Cemetery, Kennett Square, Pennsylvania
Jules DASSIN	First Cemetery, Athens, Greece
Miles DAVIS	Woodlawn Cemetery, Bronx, New York (large black tomb, tip of Alpine Section at Heather and Fir)
James DEAN	Park Cemetery, Fairmount, Indiana
Albert DEKKER (John Ecke/Ekke)	Ashes buried (unmarked) or spread at Garden State Crematory, North Bergen, New Jersey
Nelson DE LA ROSA	Cementerio de Cristo Salvador, Santo Domingo, Dominican Republic
Dino DE LAURENTIIS	Cimitero Comunale Torre Annunziata, Torre Annunziata, Naples province, Italy
Dolores DEL RIO	Ashes in Panteon de Dolores Cemetery, Mexico City
Dom DELUISE	Ashes returned to family
Jacques DEMY	Montparnasse Cemetery, Paris (9th Division)
Richard DENNING	Makawao Veterans Cemetery, Makawao, Hawaii (new section, grave 113)

Sandy DENNIS	Ashes in glass-fronted case, Lincoln Memorial Park, Lincoln, Nebraska
John DENVER	Ashes scattered over Rocky Mountains
Guillaume DEPARDIEU	Cemetery of Bougival, Yvelines, Ile de France
Patrick DEWAERE (Maurin)	Saint-Lambert-du-Lattay, Maine-et-Loire, France
Brad DEXTER	Desert Memorial Park, Cathedral City, Palm Springs, California (B-2, no. 28)
Marlene DIETRICH	Friedenau Cemetery, Schöneberg, Berlin
Albert DIEUDONNÉ (Napoleon)	Courça, Indre-et-Loire, France
Tamara DOBSON	Woodlawn Memorial Park, Baltimore, Maryland
Solveig DOMMARTIN	Cemetery of Bulgnéville Vosges, Vosges, France
Robert DONAT	Ashes scattered at St. Marylebone Crematorium, Finchley, London
Donal DONNELLY	Cremated, ashes scattered
James DOOHAN ("Scotty" of *Star Trek*)	Ashes returned to family
Françoise DORLÉAC	Cemetery of Seine-Port, Seine-et-Marne, France
Diana DORS (and Alan LAKE)	Sunningdale Cemetery, near Windsor, UK
Tommy DORSEY	Kensico Cemetery, Valhalla, New York
Paul DOUGLAS	Rose garden, St. Paul's, Covent Garden, London
Bobby DRISCOLL	Hart Island, New York (pauper's grave)
Peter DUEL (Deuel)	Oakdale Cemetery, Penfield, New York
Charles DURNING	Arlington National Cemetery, Arlington, Virginia

Harry and Daisy EARLES (*Freaks*)	Ashes scattered at sea
Johnny ECK (*Freaks*)	Greenmount Cemetery, Baltimore, Maryland
Billy ECKSTINE	Ashes returned to family
Sergei EISENSTEIN	Novodevichy Cemetery, Moscow
Duke ELLINGTON	Woodlawn Cemetery, Bronx, New York (across from Miles Davis, at tip of Wild Rose Section, two large crosses)
Denholm ELLIOT	Ashes scattered in family garden, Ibiza
Dick EMERY	Plaque at Mortlake Crematorium, London
Peg ENTWHISTLE	Ashes buried in plot of H. Milton Ross, Oak Hill Cemetery, Cincinnati, Ohio
Dale EVANS	Sunset Hills Memorial Park, Apple Valley, California
Edith EVANS	St. Paul's, Covent Garden, London
Dennis FARINA	Mount Carmel Cemetery, Hillside, Cook County, Illinois
Frances FARMER	Our Lady of Miraculous Medal Mausoleum, Oak Lawn Memorial Park, Indianapolis, Indiana
Alice FAYE	Ashes in Palm Springs Mausoleum, Cathedral City, California (east end of Mission San Luis Rey Section, behind glass, next to Phil Harris)
Federico FELLINI	Rimini, Italy
FERNANDEL	Passy Cemetery, Paris (1st division)
Jose FERRER	Santa Maria Magdalena de Pazziz Cemetery, San Juan, Puerto Rico
Mel FERRER	Ashes buried on ranch at Carpinteria, California

Barry FITZGERALD	Dean's Grange Burial Ground, Dublin, Ireland
Geraldine FITZGERALD	Woodlawn Cemetery, Bronx, New York
Gracie FIELDS	Protestant cemetery, Capri, Italy
Joan FONTAINE	Ashes scattered off Carmel Beach, California
Margot FONTEYN	Garden of Peace Memorial Park, Panama City
Bryan FORBES	Ashes scattered in garden at Virginia Water, Surrey, UK
Paul FORD	Ashes returned to family
Tennessee Ernie FORD	Ashes returned to family
John FORSYTHE	Oak Hill Cemetery, Ballard, Santa Barbara City, California
Bob FOSSE	Ashes scattered over Atlantic
Barry FOSTER	Ashes scattered at Guildford Crematorium, Surrey, UK
Elisabeth FRASER (*Bilko*)	Ashes scattered at sea
Ronald FRASER	Hampstead Cemetery, West Hampstead, London
Dolores FULLER (*Glen or Glenda*)	Palm Memorial Park, Las Vegas
Louis de FUNÈS	Le Cellier, Loire-Atlantique, France
Gert FROBE	Waldfriedhof, Icking, Bavaria
Jean GABIN	Ashes scattered over Atlantic
Abel GANCE	Auteuil Cemetery, Paris
James GANDOLFINI	Cremated
Greta GARBO	Ashes buried in forested cemetery of Skogskyrkogarden, Stockholm, Sweden
Ava GARDNER	Sunset Hills Memorial Park, Smithfield, North Carolina
John GARFIELD	Westchester Hills Cemetery, Hastings-on-Hudson, New York

Judy GARLAND	Ferncliff Cemetery, Hartsdale, New York (new wing of main mausoleum, second floor, unit 9, alcove HH, crypt 31)
Betty GARRETT	Sandy Mount United Methodist Church Cemetery, Finksburg, Maryland
Greer GARSON	Sparkman-Hillcrest Memorial Park, Dallas, Texas
Ben GAZZARA	Woodlawn Cemetery, Bronx, New York
Henry GIBSON	Ashes returned to family
Annie GIRARDOT	Père Lachaise Cemetery, Paris (49th division)
Dorothy and Lilian GISH	Ashes (with mother) in columbarium below St. Bartholomew's Church, New York, New York
Jackie GLEASON	Our Lady of Mercy Cemetery, Miami, Florida (private mausoleum)
Brian GLOVER	Brompton Cemetery, London
Paulette GODDARD	Porto Ronco, Lago Maggiore, Switzerland (next to Erich Maria Remarque)
Benny GOODMAN	Longridge Union Cemetery, Longridge, Connecticut (stone bench, on second driveway, at end of road and to right)
Ruth GORDON	Abels Hill Cemetery, Chillmark, Massachusetts
Frank GORSHIN	Calvary Cemetery, Pittsburgh, Pennsylvania
Maurice GOSFIELD (Private Duane Doberman of the *Phil Silvers Show*)	Long Island National Cemetery, Farmingdale, New York

Michael GOUGH	Ashes scattered at sea
Dulcie GRAY	Break Spear Crematorium, London
Andy GRIFFITH	Griffith Family Estate, Roanoke Island, Dare City, North Carolina
D. W. GRIFFITH	Mount Tabor Church Cemetery, Kentucky (route 22 east of Crestwood)
Kenneth GRIFFITH	Churchyard, Penally, Pembrokeshire, Wales
Richard GRIFFITHS	Holy Trinity Churchyard, Stratford-upon-Avon, UK
Sir Alec GUINNESS	Petersfield Cemetery, Petersfield, Hampshire, UK
Fred GWYNNE	Sandy Mount Cemetery, Sandy Mount, Maryland
Bill HALEY	Ashes returned to family
Margaret HAMILTON	Ashes scattered
Marvin HAMLISCH	Mt. Zion Cemetery, Maspeth, New York
Oscar HAMMERSTEIN I (impresario)	Woodlawn Cemetery, Bronx, New York (Goldenrod Section along Filbert Ave, bronze cameo on monument)
Oscar HAMMERSTEIN II (composer)	Ashes returned to family
Tony HANCOCK	Boundary wall, St. Dunstan's Churchyard, Cranford Park, London
William HANNA	Ascension Cemetery, Lake Forest, California
Sir Cedric HARDWICKE	Ashes scattered at Golders Green Crematorium, London
Phil HARRIS	Ashes inurned in Palm Springs Mausoleum, Cathedral City, California (east end of Mission San Luis Rey Section, behind glass, next to Alice Faye)

Richard HARRIS	Ashes scattered in the Bahamas
Sir Rex HARRISON	Ashes scattered in hills above San Genesio, Portofino, Italy
William S. HART	Greenwood Cemetery, Brooklyn, New York
Laurence HARVEY	Ashes buried in Santa Barbara Cemetery, Santa Barbara, California (Ocean View Addition C, grave 132, under big tree, halfway along row)
Imogen HASSALL	Gap Road Cemetery, Wimbledon, UK
Howard HAWKS	Ashes scattered
Sir Nigel HAWTHORNE	Cremated at Stevenage, UK
Charles HAWTREY	Plaque at Mortlake Crematorium, London; ashes scattered in plot 50C
Will HAY	Crematorium, Streatham Park Cemetery, Streatham Vale, London
Helen HAYES	Oak Hill Cemetery, Nyack, New York
Will HAYS	Center Ridge Cemetery, Sullivan, Indiana
Susan HAYWARD	Our Lady's Memory Garden, Cemetery of Our Lady of Perpetual Help Church, Carrollton, Georgia
Margaux HEMINGWAY	Town cemetery, Ketchum, Idaho
David HEMMINGS	St. Peter's Churchyard, Calne, UK
Sonja HENIE	Henie-Onstad Art Center, Oslo, Norway
Jim HENSON	Ashes returned to family
Audrey HEPBURN	Village cemetery, Tolochenaz, Lausanne, Lake Geneva, Switzerland
Katharine HEPBURN	Cedar Hill Cemetery, Hartford, Connecticut (section 10)
Wendy HILLER	Ashes returned to family
Earl Fatha HINES	Evergreen Cemetery, Oakland, California

Gregory HINES	St. Volodymyr's Ukrainian Catholic Cemetery, Oakville, Ontario
Gloria HOLDEN	Hillside Memorial Park, Redlands, California
Billie HOLLIDAY	St. Raymond's Cemetery, Bronx, New York (new section, St. Paul, plot 29, grave 1–2)
Judy HOLLIDAY (Tuvim)	Westchester Hills Cemetery, Hastings-on-Hudson, New York
Dennis HOPPER	Jesus Nazareno Cemetery, Ranchos de Taos, Taos City, New Mexico
Hedda HOPPER	Rosehill Cemetery, Altoona, Pennsylvania
Lena HORNE	Evergreen Cemetery, Brooklyn, New York
Harry HOUDINI (Weiss)	Macpelah Cemetery, Queens, New York
Whitney HOUSTON	Fairview Cemetery, Westfield, New Jersey
Leslie HOWARD	Plane shot down by Nazis
Trevor HOWARD	Ashes buried outside St. Peter's Church, Arkley, North London (family plaque on outer church wall)
Frankie HOWERD	St. Gregory's Churchyard, Weare, Somerset, UK
Howard HUGHES	Glenwood Cemetery, Houston, Texas
John HUGHES	Lake Forest Cemetery, Lake Forest, Illinois
Walter HUSTON	Ashes buried in Belmont Memorial Park, Fresno, California (section 702, lot 8, space 4)
Betty HUTTON	Desert Memorial Park, Palm Springs, California (B-35, lot 503)
John INMAN	Golders Green Crematorium, London

John IRELAND	Santa Barbara Cemetery, Santa Barbara, California (Mausoleum in the Pines, block C4, tier 6, crypt 9)
Burl IVES	Ashes beside mother, Mound Cemetery, Newton, Illinois
Hattie JACQUES	Putney Vale Crematorium, London (Glades of Remembrance, opposite panel 16, under oak tree)
Dean JAGGER	Resthaven Memorial Park, Modesto, California
Sid JAMES	Ashes scattered in section 2 I, Golders Green Crematorium, London
Emil JANNINGS	Sanct Wolfgang, near Strobl, Austria
Maurice JARRE	Cremated
Ben JOHNSON	City Cemetery, Pawhuska, Oklahoma
Tor JOHNSON	Eternal Valley Cemetery, Newhall, California
Raul JULIA	Buxeda Cemetery, San Juan, Puerto Rico
Curd JÜRGENS	Zentralfriedhof, Vienna (black monument with white masks)
Madeline KAHN	Ashes returned to family
Helen KANE (model for Betty Boop)	Long Island National Cemetery, New York
Boris KARLOFF	Guildford Crematorium, Guildford, UK (ashes in Garden of Remembrance, plot 2, on left, marker under rosebush)
Andy KAUFMAN	Beth David Cemetery, Elmont, New York
Danny KAYE	Kensico Cemetery, Valhalla, New York (ashes in bench monument)
Howard KEEL	Ashes scattered on a Cheshire golf course, at Lennon Airport (Liverpool, UK), and in Tuscany

Ruby KEELER (Lowe)	Holy Sepulcher Cemetery, Orange, California (section N, tier 21, grave 46).
David KELLY	Mt. Jerome Cemetery and Crematorium, Dublin, Ireland
Grace KELLY	Monaco Cathedral, Monte Carlo, Monaco
Jim KELLY	Cremated
Kay KENDALL	St. John's Churchyard, Hampstead, London
Arthur KENNEDY	Woodlawn Cemetery, Lequille, Nova Scotia, Canada.
Deborah KERR	St. Mary Churchyard, Redgrave, Suffolk
Evelyn KEYES	Santa Barbara Cemetery, Santa Barbara, California
Roy KINNEAR	East Sheen Cemetery, Richmond, Surrey, UK (plot B, grave 5)
Phyllis KIRK	Arlington National Cemetery, Arlington, Virginia
Eartha KITT	Cremated
Werner KLEMPERER (Col. Klink)	Ashes scattered at sea off Los Angeles
Jack KLUGMAN	Cremated
Werner KRAUSS	Zentralfriedhof, Vienna, Austria
Sylvia KRISTEL	Utrecht Sint-Barbara Roman Catholic Cemetery, Utrecht, Holland (plot Vak H2, rij. 1, graf. 19)
Stanley KUBRICK	Chidwickbury Manor, Hertfordshire, UK (buried in rose garden)
Nancy KULP	Ashes given to friend
Bert LAHR	Union Field Cemetery, Queens, New York (off Central Avenue, near back of cemetery, in Lahrheim-Geisenheimer family plot)

Veronica LAKE	Ashes scattered over Atlantic
Elissa LANDI	Oak Hill Cemetery, Newburyport, Massachusetts
David LEAN	Cremated at Putney Vale, London
Heath LEDGER	Fremantle Cemetery, Fremantle, Australia
Bruce and Brandon LEE	Lake View Cemetery, Seattle, Washington
Vivien LEIGH	Ashes scattered over lake at Tickerage Mill, near London
Margaret LEIGHTON	Ashes scattered at Chichester Crematorium, UK
John LE MESURIER	Ashes under square inscribed stone in corner of churchyard in Ramsgate, Kent, UK
Lotte LENYA (and Kurt Weill)	Mount Repose Cemetery, Route 9 West, Rockland County, New York
LEO (the MGM lion)	Phifer's Farm, Long Hill, Passaic Valley, thirty miles west of New York (under white pine tree, by roadside)
Richard LEPARMENTIER	Austin Memorial Park Cemetery, Austin, Texas.
Beatrice LILLIE	Harpsden, UK
Max LINDER	Saint-Loubes, France
Frederick LOEWE	Desert Memorial Park, Palm Springs, California, (B-8, lot 89)
Jack LORD	Ashes scattered on Oahu, Hawaii
Marion LORNE ("Aunt Clara" of *Bewitched*)	Ferncliff Cemetery, Hartsdale, New York (main mausoleum, unit 3 niche, panel EE, niche 10)
Linda LOVELACE (Marciano)	Parker Cemetery, Douglas City, Colorado
Arthur LOWE	Sutton Coldfield Crematorium, Birmingham, UK (ashes scattered in area DL1)

Myrna LOY	Ashes buried with parents (David Williams, 1918), Forest Vale Cemetery, Helena, Montana
Sidney LUMET	New Mount Carmel Cemetery, Glendale, New York (section 13, grave 20).
Paul LYNDE	Amity Ebenezer Baptist Church Cemetery, Amity, Ohio
Bernie MAC	Washington Memorial Gardens Cemetery, Homewood, Illinois
James MacARTHUR	Oak Hill Cemetery, Nyack, New York
Dorothy MACKAILL	Ashes scattered in Hawaii
Fulton MACKAY	East Sheen Cemetery, Richmond, Surrey, UK (JC 187, in center, near chapel)
Gordon MACRAE	Wyuka Cemetery, Lincoln, Nebraska
Jayne MANSFIELD	Fairview Cemetery, Pen Argyl, Pennsylvania
Jean MARAIS	Vallauris, France
Fredric MARCH	Firefly Farm, New Milford, Connecticut (ashes buried under tree)
Marian MARSH	Desert Memorial Park, Cathedral City, Palm Springs, California (plot B-35, site 129)
E. G. MARSHALL	Ashes returned to home, Mount Kisco, New York
Mary MARTIN	Cemetery, Weatherford, Texas (with parents and husband Richard Halliday)
Lee MARVIN	Arlington Cemetery, Arlington, Virginia
Harpo MARX	Ashes supposedly scattered at 7th hole of Rancho Mirage Golf Course, Palm Springs, California
James MASON	Cemetery, Corsier-sur-Vevey, Lac Leman, Switzerland (just left of Chaplin)

Raymond MASSEY	Ashes buried in Beaverdale Memorial Park, New Haven, Connecticut (Ludington plot)
Marcello MASTROIANNI	Verano Cemetery, Rome
Jessie MATTHEWS	Churchyard of St. Martin's, Ruislip, UK
Victor MATURE	St. Michael's Catholic Cemetery, Louisville, Kentucky
Lois MAXWELL	Cremated
Virginia MAYO	Valley Oaks Memorial Park, Westlake Village, California (Garden of Gethsemane, plot 313)
Joel McCREA	Ashes scattered over the Pacific
T. P. MCKENNA	Mullagh Parish Church, Mullagh, City Cavan, Ireland
Donald MEEK	Fairmount Cemetery, Denver, Colorado (crypt in mausoleum)
Marianagela MELATO	Cremated
Melina MERCOURI	First Cemetery, Athens, Greece
Una MERKEL	Highland Cemetery, Fort Mitchell, Kentucky
Ethel MERMAN	Shrine of Remembrance Mausoleum, Colorado Springs, Colorado (memorial plaque above daughter's crypt; ashes returned to family)
Russ MEYER	Stockton Rural Cemetery, Stockton, California
Ray MILLAND	Ashes scattered at sea
Spike MILLIGAN	St. Thomas's Church, Winchelsea, East Sussex, UK
Mary MILLINGTON	Mortlake Catholic Cemetery, St. Mary Magdalene's Churchyard, Mortlake, London (horizontal slab under name of mother, Joan Quilter)

Sir John MILLS	St. Mary's Churchyard, Denham, Buckinghamshire, UK
Sal MINEO	Gate of Heaven Cemetery, Hawthorne, New York (flush plaque near back, section S, not far from road)
Anthony MINGHELLA	Cremated at Golders Green, London
Carmen MIRANDA	Sâo Joâo Batista Cemetery, Rio de Janeiro, Brazil (red granite mausoleum, with statue of St. Anthony)
Cameron MITCHELL	Desert Memorial Park, Palm Springs, California (A-23, no. 83)
Yves MONTAND	Père Lachaise Cemetery, Paris
Hugo MONTENEGRO	Wellwood Murray Cemetery, Palm Springs, California (11-3, no. G)
Maria MONTEZ	Montparnasse Cemetery, Paris
Dudley MOORE	Hillside Cemetery, Scotch Plains, New Jersey
Agnes MOOREHEAD	Dayton Memorial Park Cemetery Abbey, Dayton, Ohio
Kenneth MORE	Putney Vale Crematorium, London (ashes possibly scattered)
Eric MORECAMBE	Church of St. Nicholas, Harpenden, Hertfordshire, UK (ashes scattered in Garden of Remembrance)
Dennis MORGAN (Stanley Morner)	Oak Hill District Cemetery, Oakhurst, California
Frank MORGAN	Greenwood Cemetery, Brooklyn, New York
Robert MORLEY	St. Mary's Churchyard, Wargrave, Berkshire, UK
Jim MORRISON	Père Lachaise Cemetery, Paris
Zero MOSTEL	Ashes scattered
Ona MUNSON (*Gone with the Wind*)	Ferncliff Cemetery, Hartsdale, New York

Nita NALDI	Calvary Cemetery, Woodside, New York
Charles NAPIER	Bakersfield National Cemetery, Arvin, Kern City, California (section A, row D, site 15)
Anna NEAGLE (and Herbert WILCOX)	City of London Cemetery, Aldersbrook Road, London
Patricia NEAL	Abbey of Regina Laudis, Bethlehem, Connecticut
Pola NEGRI	San Antonio, Texas
Barry NELSON	Greenwood Cemetery, Hulmeville, Pennsylvania
Anthony NEWLEY	Forest Hills Memorial Park, Palm City, Florida
Robert NEWTON	Ashes in friends' wine cellar, Brighton, UK
Leslie NIELSEN	Evergreen Cemetery, Fort Lauderdale, Florida
Harry NILSSON	Valley Oaks Memorial Park, Westlake Village, California
David NIVEN	Chateau d'Oex, Switzerland
Philippe NOIRET	Montparnasse, Paris (Avenue Transversale, 3rd division, 1st section)
Rudolf NUREYEV	Sainte-Geneviève des Bois, near Paris
Warren OATES	Ashes to Packard, Kentucky
Pascale OGIER	Père-Lachaise, Paris (52nd division)
Laurence OLIVIER	Westminster Abbey, London
Milo O'SHEA	Deansgrange Cemetery, Blackrock, Dublin, Ireland
Maureen O'SULLIVAN	Most Holy Redeemer Cemetery, Niskayuna, New York
Peter O'TOOLE	cremated
Bill OWEN	St. John's Churchyard, Upperthong, Yorkshire, UK
Reginald OWEN	Morris Hill Cemetery, Boise, Idaho

G. W. PABST	Zentralfriedhof, Vienna, Austria
Anita PAGE	Holy Cross Cemetery, San Diego, California
Alan PAKULA	Green River Cemetery, East Hampton, New York
Eugene PALLETTE	Greenfield Cemetery, Grenola, Kansas (ashes unmarked in parents' plot)
Dorothy PARKER	National Association for the Advancement of Colored People (NAACP), Baltimore, Maryland (ashes buried)
Fess PARKER	Santa Barbara Cemetery, Santa Barbara, California
John PAYNE	Ashes scattered in Norfolk, Virginia
George PEPPARD	North View Cemetery, Dearborn, Michigan
Jon PERTWEE	Cremated at Putney Vale, London
River PHOENIX	Gainesville, Florida
Slim PICKENS	Modesto, California
Marie-France PISIER	Cemetery of Sanary-sur-Mer, France
Ingrid PITT	East Sheen and Richmond Cemetery, Richmond, London (section 16, grave 2043)
Donald PLEASANCE	Cremated at Putney Vale, London
Carlo PONTI	Cimitero di Magenta, Lombardia, Italy
Pete POSTLETHWAITE	Buried near Bishop's Castle, Shropshire, UK
Michael POWELL	Holy Cross Church, Avening, UK
William POWELL	Desert Memorial Park, Palm Springs, California (section B-10, lot 20)
Otto PREMINGER	Cremation niche, Chapel Mausoleum B, Azelia Room, Woodlawn, New York
Elvis PRESLEY	Graceland, Memphis, Tennessee
Marie PREVOST	Ashes returned to family
Dennis PRICE	St. Peter's Church, Sark, UK

Lya de PUTTI	Ferncliff Cemetery, Hartsdale, New York (main mausoleum, first floor)
Mae QUESTEL (Betty Boop/Olive Oyl)	New Montefiore Cemetery, Farmingdale, New York
Anthony QUINN	Buried on his private estate, Bristol, Rhode Island
Sergei RACHMANINOFF	Kensico Cemetery, Valhalla, New York
Gilda RADNER	Longridge Union Cemetery, Longridge, Connecticut (stone bench, near middle of Benny Goodman section)
Claude RAINS	Red Hill Cemetery, Moultonborough, New Hampshire
Basil RATHBONE	Ferncliff Cemetery, Hartsdale, New York (Shrine of Memories Mausoleum)
Johnny RAY	Hopewell Cemetery, Yamhill County, Oregon
Martha RAYE	Post Cemetery, Fort Bragg, North Carolina
Ronald and Nancy REAGAN	Reagan Library and Museum, Simi Valley, Thousand Oaks, California
Corin REDGRAVE	Cremated
Lynn REDGRAVE	St. Peter's Episcopal Cemetery, Lithgow, New York
Michael REDGRAVE	St. Paul's, Covent Garden, London (ashes buried in garden)
Carol REED	Gunnersbury Cemetery, London
Oliver REED	Churchyard in Churchtown, Ireland
Christopher REEVE	Ashes returned to family
Jim REEVES	Jim Reeves Memorial Park, Carthage, Texas
Steve REEVES	Ashes scattered in Montana
Michael RENNIE	Harlow Hill Cemetery, Harrogate, Yorkshire, UK (grave F21)

Jean RENOIR	Essoyes, Aube, France
Fernando REY	Cementerio de la Almudena, Madrid, Spain.
Alicia RHETT	St. Philips Episcopal Church cemetery, Charleston, Sth Carolina
Wendy RICHARD	East Finchley Cemetery and Crematorium, London
Ian RICHARDSON	Royal Shakespeare Theatre, Stratford-on-Avon, UK (ashes in foundation of auditorium)
Natasha RICHARDSON	St. Peter's Episcopal Cemetery, Lithgow, New York
Ralph RICHARDSON	Highgate Cemetery East, London
Leni RIEFENSTAHL	Waldfriedhof (Ostfriedhof), Munich
Hal ROACH G	Woodlawn Cemetery, Elmira, New York
Jason ROBARDS	Cremated
Marty ROBBINS	Woodlawn Cemetery, Nashville, Tennessee
Rachel ROBERTS	Ashes scattered over River Thames, London
Cliff ROBERTSON	Cedar Lawn Cemetery, East Hampton, New York
Paul ROBESON	Ferncliff Cemetery, Hartsdale, New York
Dany ROBIN (and Michael Sullivan)	Montfort-l'Amaury, Yvelines, France
Bill "Bojangles" ROBINSON	Evergreen Cemetery, Brooklyn, New York
Edward G. ROBINSON	Beth El Cemetery, Glendale, New York (Goodman Mausoleum, top right)
Flora ROBSON	Ashes at St. Nicholas Churchyard, Brighton, UK
Richard RODGERS	Ashes in unidentified space at Ferncliff Cemetery, Hartsdale, New York

Charles "Buddy" ROGERS	Forest Lawn Palm Springs Mausoleum, Cathedral City, Palm Springs, California (east end of Mission Santa Rosa block, just below Jane Wyman)
Roy ROGERS	Sunset Hills Memorial Park, Apple Valley, California
Will ROGERS	Will Rogers Memorial, Claremore, Oklahoma
Ruth ROMAN	Ashes scattered at sea
Margaret RUTHERFORD	St. James's Churchyard, Gerrards Cross, Buckinghamshire, UK
Robert RYAN	Lampell Farm, Flemington, New Jersey (ashes buried beside a pear tree)
George SANDERS	Ashes scattered over English Channel
Michael SARRAZIN	Notre-Dame-des-Neiges Cemetery, Montreal, Quebec
Maria SCHELL	Ortsfriedhof, Preitenegg, Wolfsberg Bezirk, Kärnten, Austria
Maximilian SCHELL	Zentralfriedhof, Vienna, Austria
Joe and Nick SCHENK	Maimonides Cemetery, Brooklyn, New York
Rosanna SCHIAFFINO	Cemetery of the Borgo, Portofino, Liguria, Italy
Maria SCHNEIDER	Ashes scattered in Biarritz, France
Romy SCHNEIDER	Boissy-sans-Avoir, France (behind little church)
Max SCHRECK	Wilmersdorfer Waldfriedhof, Berlin
Paul SCOFIELD	St. Mary's Churchyard, Balcombe, West Sussex, UK
Gordon SCOTT	Kensico Cemetery, Valhalla, New York
Martha SCOTT	Masonic Cemetery, Jamesport, Missouri
Randolph SCOTT	Elmwood Cemetery, Charlotte, North Carolina

Terry SCOTT	Unknown cemetery in Godalming, Surrey, UK
Jean SEBERG	Montparnasse Cemetery, Paris
Harry SECOMBE	Ashes buried (marked by stone) in Shamley Green Churchyard, between Guildford and Cranleigh, Surrey, UK
Edie SEDGWICK (Post)	Oak Hill Cemetery, Ballard, California
Peter SELLERS	Golders Green Crematorium, London
Larry SEMON	Philadelphia, Pennsylvania (family plot)
Rod SERLING	Lakeview Cemetery, Interlaken, New York
Michel SERRAULT	Cimetière Sainte Catherine (Honfleur), Calvados, France
David SEVILLE (Chipmunks)	Ararat Cemetery, Fresno, California (ashes under WWII marker)
Delphine SEYRIG	Montparnasse Cemetery, Paris
Del SHANNON	Ashes scattered in California desert
Artie SHAW	Valley Oaks Memorial Park, Westlake Village, California
Robert SHAW	Ashes scattered near home in Ireland
Moira SHEARER	Durisdeer Cemetery, Durisdeer, Scotland
Dinah SHERIDAN	Northwood Cemetery, Northwood, London
Don SIEGEL	Ashes at Cayucos Morrow Bay Cemetery, Cayucos, California
Simone SIGNORET	Père Lachaise Cemetery, Paris
Ron SILVER	Westchester Hills Cemetery, Hastings-on-Hudson, New York (block J)
Jay SILVERHEELS (Harold Smith)	Flags Indian Reservation, Brandford, Ontario
Alastair SIM	Body left to medical research
Joan SIMS	Cremated at Putney Vale, London

Frank SINATRA	Desert Memorial Park, Cathedral City, Palm Springs, California (Da Vall Road, off Ramon Road, near entrance, by left edge of main lawn, next to parents, B-8, lot 151)
Walter and Leo SLEZAK	Rotach-Egern village cemetery, Bavaria
Anna Nicole SMITH	Lakeview Cemetery, Nassau, Bahamas
Sam SPIEGEL	Beth Olom Cemetery, Queens, New York
Barbara STANWYCK	Ashes scattered over Lone Pine, California
Maureen STAPLETON	St. Mary's Cemetery, Troy, New York
Anna STEN	Cremated
Leopold STOKOWSKI	St. Marylebone Cemetery, London
Johnny STOMPANATO	National Veterans Cemetery outside Chicago, Illinois
Lewis STONE	Ashes scattered at Malibu ranch
Lee and Paula STRASBERG	Westchester Hills Cemetery, Hastings-on-Hudson, New York
Woody STRODE	Military cemetery, Riverside, California
Erich von STROHEIM	Maurepas Cemetery, Les Yvelines, France
Preston STURGES	Ferncliff Cemetery, Hartsdale, New York (outside Shrine of Memories Mausoleum)
Jule STYNE	Mt. Ararat Cemetery, Farmingdale, New York
Margaret SULLAVAN	St. Mary's Whitechapel Churchyard, Lancaster, Virginia
Donna SUMMER	Harpeth Hills Memory Gardens, Nashville, Tennessee (Garden of Faith Section)
Gloria SWANSON	Church of the Heavenly Rest, New York, New York (columbarium)

Patrick SWAYZE	Ashes scattered on his New Mexico ranch
Blanche SWEET	Brooklyn Botanic Garden, New York (ashes around lilac bush named after her)
Jessica TANDY	Ashes returned to family
Jacques TATI	Cimetière Ancien, Saint-Germain-en-Laye, France (Carré H)
John THAW	Cremated at Westerleigh, Gloucestershire, UK
Terry-THOMAS	Ashes scattered
Sybil THORNDIKE	Westminster Abbey, London
Gene TIERNEY	Glenwood Cemetery, Houston, Texas
David TOMLINSON	Buried in garden of Buckinghamshire home, UK
Mike TODD	Was in Waldheim/Forest Home Cemetery, Forest Park, Illinois; location now unknown
Richard TODD	Ashes scattered in the UK
Thelma TODD	Bellevue Cemetery, Lawrence, Massachusetts
Franchot TONE	Ashes scattered in Canada, probably at Niagara Falls
Mary TRAVERS	Umpawaug Cemetery, Reading, Connecticut
Marie TRINTIGNANT	Père Lachaise Cemetery, Paris
François TRUFFAUT	Montmartre Cemetery, Paris
Sophie TUCKER	Emanuel Cemetery, Wethersfield, Connecticut
Sonny TUFTS	Lexington Cemetery, Lexington, Massachusetts (Westfall Section)
Lana TURNER	Ashes possibly scattered in Hawaii
Peter USTINOV	Bursins Cemetery, Nyon, Switzerland
Roger VADIM	St. Tropez, France
Alida VALLI	Cimitero del Verano, Rome

James VAN HEUSEN	Desert Memorial Park, Palm Springs, California (B-8, lot 63, near Frank Sinatra)
Lupe VELEZ	Panteon de Dolores, Mexico City
Lino VENTURA	Val-Saint-Germain, 91-Essonne, France
Gwen VERDON	Ashes taken to New York
King VIDOR	Ashes buried on Willow Creek Ranch, near San Luis Obispo, California
Jacques VILLERET	Cimetière de Perrusson, Loches, France
Gene VINCENT	Eternal Valley Cemetery, Newhall, California
Robert WALKER	Washington Heights Cemetery, Ogden, Utah
Fats WALLER	Ashes scattered over Harlem, New York
Raoul WALSH	Assumption Catholic Cemetery, Simi Valley, California (section B, tier 28, grave 40)
Simon WARD	Ashes scattered at sea
Johnny WEISSMULLER	Acapulco, Mexico
Orson WELLES	Ashes buried in well on a friend's farm, Ronda, Spain
Mae WEST	Cypress Hills Cemetery, Brooklyn, New York (Abbey Mausoleum, second floor, aisle EE, crypt 1)
Carol WHITE	Mortlake Cemetery, London (ashes buried with parents)
Pearl WHITE	Passy Cemetery, Paris
Wilfrid Hyde WHITE	Ashes buried in Bourton-on-the-Water Cemetery, UK
Richard WIDMARK	Laurel Hill Cemetery, Soco, Maine
Jack WILD	Toddington Parish Cemetery, Toddington, Bedfordshire, UK (new section)

Brian WILDE	Harwood Park Crematorium, Tring, Hertsfordshire, UK
Michael WILDING	Ashes scattered at Chichester Crematorium, UK
Kenneth WILLIAMS	St. Marylebone Crematorium, East Finchley Cemetery, London.
Tennessee WILLIAMS	Calvary Cemetery, St. Louis, Missouri
Tex WILLIAMS	Eternal Valley Cemetery, Newhall, California
Nicol WILLIAMSON	Cremated
Jackie WILSON	Westlawn Cemetery, Wayne, Michigan
Michael WINNER	Willesden United Synagogue Cemetery, Willesden, London
Norman WISDOM	Bride Church Cemetery, Bride, Isle of Man
Googie WITHERS	Ashes scattered at sea
Edward WOODWARD	Padstow Cemetery, Padstow, Cornwall, UK
Jane WYMAN	Forest-Lawn Cathedral City, Palm Springs, California (lot 5F, east end of Mission Santa Rosa Block)
Patrick WYMARK	Highgate West Cemetery, London, UK (just right of entrance)
Dick YORK	Plainfield Township Cemetery, Rockford, Michigan
Susannah YORK	Ashes scattered on Paxos beach, Greece, and in the garden of her former home in Wandsworth, UK
Gig YOUNG (Byron Barr)	Ashes sent to Barr family plot, Waynesville, North Carolina
Florenz ZIEGFELD (and Billie BURKE)	Kensico Cemetery, Valhalla, New York (under willow at end of Powhatan Avenue)

References

Alleman, R. 1985. *The Movie Lover's Guide to Hollywood*. New York: Harper Colophon.

Bifulco, M. 2012. Publicity Makes a Prophet Profitable, in *Pop Twenty no. 2. Twentieth-Century Pop Culture: Movies—TV—Radio—Music*, M. J. Bifulco and R. S. Birchard, eds. Charleston, SC, 83–106.

Birchard, R. S. 1991. "The Making of *The Squaw Man*." *Shadowland: Journal of the Hollywood Studio Museum* 1 (1): 6–9.

Brosnan, P. 1991. "Ten Commandments Set Resurrected." *Shadowland: Journal of the Hollywood Studio Museum* 1 (1): 20–21.

Brownlow, K. 1979. *Hollywood: The Pioneers*. London: Collins.

Carpenter, E. H. 1973. *Early Cemeteries of the City of Los Angeles*. Los Angeles: Dawson's Book Shop.

Culbertson, J., and Randall, T. 1989. *Permanent Californians*. Chelsea, VT: Chelsea Green Publishing Company, New York.

Ellenberger, A. R. 2001. *Celebrities in Los Angeles Cemeteries: A Directory*. Jefferson, NC: McFarland and Company, New York.

Goldstein, S. 2009. *LA's Graveside Companion: Where the V.I.P.s R.I.P.* Atglen, PA: Schiffer Publishing.

Heizer, R. F., and Elsasser, A. B. 1980. *The Natural World of the California Indians.* Berkeley: University of California Press.

Hyland, J. 2008. *The Legendary Estates of Beverly Hills.* New York: Rizzoli.

Jefferson, G. T. 1992. "People and the Brea: A Brief History of a Natural Resource." *Terra* 31 (1): 3–9.

Johnson, K. E. 1991. "Setting the Stage: Southern California and the Coming of Film." *Shadowland: Journal of the Hollywood Studio Museum* 1 (1): 22–25.

Keister, D. 2010. *Forever L.A.: A Field Guide to Los Angeles Area Cemeteries and Their Residents.* Layton, UT: Gibbs Smith.

Kobal, J. 1985. *Hollywood: The Years of Innocence.* London: Thames and Hudson.

Lamparski, R. 1981. *Lamparski's Hidden Hollywood.* New York: Fireside.

Salls, R. 1992. "Ancient Brea People." *Terra* 31 (1): 10–11.

Schessler, K. 1984. *This Is Hollywood: An Unusual Movieland Guide.* La Verne, CA: Ken Schessler Productions.

Stock, C. 1956. *Rancho La Brea. A Record of Pleistocene Life in California.* Los Angeles County Museum of Natural History Science Series no. 20, Paleontology no. 11, 6th edition.

Torrence, B. T. 1979. *Hollywood: The First 100 Years.* Hollywood, CA: Hollywood Chamber of Commerce.

Wallace, D. 2001. *Lost Hollywood.* New York: LA Weekly Books.

Williams, G. P. 2011. *The Story of Hollywood: An Illustrated History.* Austin, TX: BL Press.

$\mathcal{I}_{n\,d\,e\,x}$

About the Author

Paul G. Bahn (M.A., Ph.D., F.S.A.) was born and raised in Hull, England; studied archaeology at the University of Cambridge; and did his Ph.D. thesis (1979) on the prehistory of the French Pyrenees. He then held postdoctoral fellowships at Liverpool and London, plus a J. Paul Getty postdoctoral fellowship in the History of Art and the Humanities. Since going freelance in the mid-1980s, he has devoted himself to writing, editing, and translating books on archaeology, plus occasional journalism and as much travel as possible. His main research interest is prehistoric art, especially rock art of the world, and most notably Paleolithic art, as well as the art of Easter Island. He led the team which, at his instigation, searched for and discovered the first Ice Age cave art in Britain in 2003 and 2004.

Among his written or cowritten books are *Pyrenean Prehistory* (1984); *Ancient Places* (with Glyn Daniel, 1986); *Images of the Ice Age* (with Jean Vertut, 1988); *The Bluffer's Guide to Archaeology* (4th ed., 2007); *Archaeology: Theories, Methods and*

Practice (with Colin Renfrew, 6th ed., 2012); *Easter Island, Earth Island* (with John Flenley, third ed., 2012); *Mammoths* (with Adrian Lister, third ed., 2007); *Archaeology: A Very Short Introduction* (second ed., 2012); *Journey through the Ice Age* (with Jean Vertut, 1997); *The Cambridge Illustrated History of Prehistoric Art* (1998); *Disgraceful Archaeology* (with Bill Tidy, second ed., 2012); *The Enigmas of Easter Island* (with John Flenley, 2003); *Cave Art: A Guide to the Decorated Ice Age Caves of Europe* (second ed., 2012); *Britain's Oldest Art: The Ice Age Cave Art of Creswell Crags* (with Paul Pettitt, 2009); *Prehistoric Rock Art: Polemics and Progress* (2010); *Dirty Diggers, or Tales from the Archaeological Trenches* (with Bill Tidy, 2013); *Archaeology Essentials* (with Colin Renfrew, third ed., 2014); *Images of the Ice Age* (2014); and one non-archaeological book, *The Cambridge Rapist* (2012).